ABSOLUTELY NASTY® CROSSWORDS

LEVEL 2

EDITED BY STANLEY NEWMAN

D1401159

PUZZLE
WRIGHT
PRESS

New York

CONTENTS

Introduction
3

Puzzles
5

Answers
148

**PUZZLE
WRIGHT
PRESS**

New York

An Imprint of Sterling Publishing
387 Park Avenue South
New York, NY 10016

PUZZLEWRIGHT PRESS, Absolutely Nasty, and the distinctive Puzzlewright Press logo
are registered trademarks of Sterling Publishing Co., Inc.

The puzzles in this book previously appeared in *Superhard Crosswords to Keep You Sharp* and
Ultrahard Crosswords to Keep You Sharp © 2010 by Stanley Newman, *Random House Ultrahard Crosswords,
Volume 1* © 1994 by Stanley Newman, *Random House Ultrahard Crosswords, Volume 2*
© 1995 by Stanley Newman, and originally appeared in *Newsday* or *Tough Puzzles*

ISBN 978-1-4549-0060-3

Distributed in Canada by Sterling Publishing
C/o Canadian Manda Group, 165 Dufferin Street
Toronto, Ontario, Canada M6K 3H6
Distributed in the United Kingdom by GMC Distribution Services
Castle Place, 166 High Street, Lewes, East Sussex, England BN7 1XU
Distributed in Australia by Capricorn Link (Australia) Pty. Ltd.
P.O. Box 704, Windsor, NSW 2756, Australia

For information about custom editions, special sales, premium and
corporate purchases, please contact Sterling Special Sales
Department at 800-805-5489 or specialsales@sterlingpublishing.com.

Manufactured in China

2   4   6   8   10   9   7   5   3   1

www.puzzlewright.com

INTRODUCTION

Welcome to *Absolutely Nasty Crosswords Level 2*, which contains some of the most difficult puzzles ever put between two covers. If you've mastered the crosswords in your local newspaper and can solve the puzzles in other crossword books as fast as you can write, you'll find the puzzles here a refreshing change.

What makes these crosswords so tough? None of the puzzles have themes, so there are no unifying elements among the answers. There are more long words and fewer short words than usual, making it more difficult to "break into" each puzzle. The puzzles cover the broadest range of factual information, and have a generous helping of devious clues. And the remaining clues have been crafted to minimize the usefulness of your dictionary as a solving aid.

For their help in the preparation of this book, I would like to thank Peter Gordon, my Puzzlewright Press editor, and Dan Feyer, for his thorough proofreading of the manuscript.

Your comments on any aspect of this book are most welcome. You can reach me via regular mail at the address below.

If you're Internet-active, you can reach me electronically through my Web site: www.StanXwords.com, which features prize contests, puzzlemaker profiles, solving hints and other fun stuff for crossword fans. Please drop by for a visit.

Best wishes for happy solving!

—Stan Newman
P.O. Box 69,
Massapequa, NY 11762
(Please enclose a self-addressed,
stamped envelope if you'd like a reply.)

ACROSS

1 It's often drawn
10 Looks at
15 In a different way
16 Dwight's opponent
17 Points in a new direction
18 Crowds' cries
19 Seashore recess
20 Tropical fish
22 Part of IRS
23 *Meet John* ___ (Capra film)
24 Made a nasal appraisal
26 CLXVII × VI
27 Prefix for while
29 Gardner et al.
30 *The Magic Mountain* author
31 Multi-vol. lexicon
33 Turn away
35 Kind of tank
38 Marchers of song
39 Hot winds
41 Sock part
42 Explorer Tasman
43 Tickle
45 Dully colored
49 Turn down
50 Most cool
52 Nabokov novel
53 Half of 26-Across, plus L
54 Give ___ (care)
55 AMPAS award
57 Corrode
59 Taking umbrage at
61 Metric measure
62 Coming-out
63 Conducts experiments
64 *The Benny Goodman Story* star

DOWN

1 Heat-resistant compound
2 *Lend Me* ___
3 Oarlock pins
4 Where "you are"
5 Formal orders
6 Reaction to Stonehenge
7 One of the hue crew
8 Sophia on *The Golden Girls*
9 Antsy
10 Electrical unit
11 Whoop-de-doo
12 Insurance payment recipient
13 W-2 data
14 Chapel of fame
21 Puts differently
25 Patient assistance program
28 Filmdom's Tevye
30 Lionlike
32 List ender: Abbr.
34 First word in three John
   Wayne film titles
35 Say "sassafras"
36 Religious recluses
37 Held a candle (to)
39 Most down
40 Person in power
44 Breath-freshener brand
46 *Phèdre* playwright
47 "Ten Cents ___" (Rodgers
   tune)
48 Crashed (in)
50 Can't stomach
51 Polynesian kingdom
56 -ist relative
58 Cleverness
60 Ending for west

1

BY TRIP PAYNE

ACROSS

1 Nick's costar in *The Deep*
11 Etcher's substance
15 Ridiculous
16 Scourge
17 Bosch paintings
18 As far as
19 Beer buy
20 Old Testament bk.
21 *Pou* ___ (vantage point)
22 Prince of opera
24 Natalie's partner in a '91 tune
26 Exceptionally
27 Uncle of song
28 Midway's home, for short
29 Elevated homes
31 Cycle starter
32 Beavers, for instance
35 FDR measure
36 Kind of pron.
37 Majestic
38 Actor Penn of *House*
39 Two-way preposition
40 Video giant, once
41 One of the earth's quadrillion
42 Singing Sergeant
44 CO clock setting
45 Sgt., e.g.
46 Calendar abbr.
47 Heat, in a way
48 Chuck Yeager's rank upon retirement: Abbr.
49 Election winners
50 Unhappiness
52 Circular dance
54 Makes lawn repairs
55 Opera manager
59 Corporeal joint
60 Candy box features
61 Conversation filler
62 Mentors, maybe

DOWN

1 Machine shop fixture
2 Part of ETA
3 Hogan's hero
4 Persian Gulf country
5 Western Indians
6 Jacket style
7 He speaks: Latin abbr.
8 Aleut language
9 Stirling negatives
10 *Lohengrin* character
11 Sadist
12 Keeshan character
13 D.W. Griffith classic
14 ___ *volente*
22 Becomes accustomed (to)
23 Tree branches of a sort
25 Attachés
26 Be in a huff about
28 Longs for
29 Planetary envelope
30 California's ___ Sea
33 Superlative suffix
34 Bellini opera
43 Renter
47 The unfunny Marx
48 Neighbor's kids
50 Thin streak
51 Lag b'___ (Hebrew holiday)
53 She-bears, in Bolivia
54 Albertville gear
56 U.K. fliers
57 Sale tag abbr.
58 CIA's forerunner

2

BY WAYNE R. WILLIAMS

ACROSS

1 Makes messy
8 Frat letter
13 Hippomenes beat her
15 Four of a kind
16 Well-meaning sort
17 Limb preceder
18 One way to go
19 Obsolete computer devices
21 The computer industry: Abbr.
22 Acrobat's workplace
24 Simulates
25 Soccer prop
26 *Damn Yankees* character
28 Blood components
29 Rhyme for mealy
30 Genesis wife
32 American juniper
34 Goddess invoked by Professor Marvel
36 Grounds for a suit
37 Free lodging
41 Aching spots
44 LaRue of films
45 Coalition
47 French philosopher Auguste
49 FBI worker
50 Candy box choice
52 Clerihew, for one
53 Letter abbr.
54 Pause
56 Pod opening
57 *Hook* extra
59 Sexy
61 Zola et al.
62 Four-time Wimbledon winner
63 Hall offerings
64 "Wait a minute!"

DOWN

1 Leadfoot catchers
2 Idyllic places
3 Deep red
4 Mideast org.
5 Landlocked land
6 The ___ the line
7 Cordwood measures
8 Horton's creator
9 Morticia's cousin
10 Cried out, in a way
11 ANC figure
12 Plug in a travel kit
14 More affected
15 Midwest menaces
20 Snow-white bird
23 Loud
27 *One Touch of Venus* lyricist
29 Superfluous
31 Ilia
33 Scaled swimmer, for short
35 Port-___ cheese
37 Showed approval
38 Cagney's final feature film
39 Oregon city
40 Mark, as a page
42 Hammy
43 Less yielding
46 Author Castaneda
48 Political fleer
50 Marquee words
51 Spanish squiggle
55 Slipper type
58 Lock, stock, and barrel
60 Sidelines cry

3

BY TRIP PAYNE

ACROSS

1 Eye annoyances
6 Riverboat gambler
15 To pieces
16 Too ready
17 Itch cause, perhaps
18 Indispensable
19 Unaffiliated: Abbr.
20 ___ Animals (cookie brand)
22 Sylvester, to Tweety Bird
23 Whoppers
25 Wise ones
26 Benefit
27 Permanent places
29 Rubber base
30 *Broken Arrow* star
31 Grating
33 Haberdashery department
35 Cries, in a way
36 Got at
40 Bedevils
44 Ride effortlessly
45 Crime-and-punishment statutes
47 English composer
48 Wooden shoe
49 Brows do it
50 Twaddle
51 Sugar product
53 Toward the stern
54 Sweetheart
56 Time limit word
58 Set off
59 Time allowance
60 Desolation
61 Makes lighter

DOWN

1 "Waltzing ___"
2 Court ruling
3 Two-seaters
4 Afore
5 Wild guess
6 Garner
7 Gets back for
8 What bands may take
9 Taps on the table
10 Six, in Seville
11 Holds
12 Shake up
13 Won back
14 Dubious reason
21 Nepalese, for instance
24 Pedigreed pet
26 Comics soldier
28 High point
29 Suit grounds
32 Take turns
34 Split
36 Ticks, e.g.
37 Fancy headband
38 Bach work
39 Campaign programs
41 Piano pieces
42 Big building
43 Comes to terms
46 Itinerants
48 Wrap session material
51 Hit on the head
52 Gravity-powered vehicle
55 African nation: Abbr.
57 New Deal agcy.

4

BY WAYNE R. WILLIAMS

ACROSS

1 Eastwood film of '88
5 More sage
10 Refrain starter
13 Prevention dosage
14 Out of the way
15 Scale notes
16 Important numbers
19 Cakes' partner
20 Fond du ___, Wisconsin
21 Intersection figure
22 NBA nickname
24 Treaty town of 1814
26 With 30-Across, elegant style
27 Stamp buys
29 German direction
30 See 26-Across
31 Naiveté personified
36 Harmfully
37 "If I can make ___ ..."
38 Rosemary portrayer in '68
39 Benefits from hard work
42 Giant syllable
43 WWII area
44 Falafel holders
45 L. Victoria's locale
46 Loses sleep (over)
48 Canine comment
49 Hurried
51 Ground + grass
53 ___ Man Answers
55 Exemplars of precision
58 72, often
59 Old Aegean region
60 Remiss
61 Mos. and mos.
62 Went through
63 Highlands wear

DOWN

1 Ready for construction
2 Richard Gere film of '90
3 Letters high above NYC, once
4 Farmer's place
5 Hellman play
6 "The Gentleman ___ Dope" (Rodgers tune)
7 Undergo a grilling
8 Proclamation
9 Sack out
10 Off on a tangent?
11 Scout's job
12 Special interest gp.
13 Eggs: Latin
17 Drop, in a way
18 Not spoken of
23 One of Bush 41's sons
25 Art lover
27 Put together
28 Richter reading
30 Annoying nerd
32 Former telecommunications co.
33 Gaslight, for one
34 Alienate
35 H.S. exams
40 Engine sounds
41 Through
45 Hosni's predecessor
46 Camera setting
47 What bureaucrats follow: Abbr.
49 Cosby series
50 "The hand that made ___ divine": Paine
52 It may be floppy
54 Invite
56 Least: Abbr.
57 Old Testament judge

5

by Randolph Ross

ACROSS

1 Housing
9 Eth.'s loc.
12 Iffy
14 Great time
17 Ready to snap
18 Northwest city
19 *The Avengers* character
20 Do a number
21 Sect suffix
22 Make changes to
24 Greek peak
26 Howard and Nessen
27 French pronoun
28 Fire man?
30 *Purple Rain* performer
32 Mag. execs
33 First section of a Hebrew dictionary
34 ___ Pieces (candy)
35 "No problem!"
37 Fred Flintstone's buddy
40 Dagger handle
41 Relief preceder
44 In the area
45 Choice word
46 False front
47 Look amused
48 Fill to the max
50 Gift getter
52 Coats, in a way
54 Knight's group
56 See
57 French spa
58 High-strung
60 Word form for "tooth"
61 Treat sacrilegiously
62 Catch on to
63 Called attention to

DOWN

1 "Don't ___" (off-the-record intro)
2 Anonymous
3 Mel Harris, Michael Learned, or Sean Young
4 Old-time stage star Ada
5 Italian cardinal
6 Hot times in Le Havre
7 Hams
8 Contemporary characteristics
9 Statesman Eban
10 Snowed slightly
11 K follower
13 What photogs used to file
15 Golfer's concern
16 Verb forms
23 Make numb
25 Spring times
29 London underwriters
31 Let out
35 Overwhelm
36 Highway marker
37 Helped at the checkout
38 Make it
39 Stirring up
41 Crazy
42 Plastic sheet
43 Became resolute
49 Talked like
51 Olfactory input
53 Annoyed state
55 Suffix for hip or tip
59 Water cooler

6

by Randolph Ross

ACROSS

1 Gaza Strip residents
6 Forwent fidgeting
14 Esther of *Good Times*
15 Ship in the news in '15
16 Let up
17 Spellbound
18 Computerese acronym
19 Ninja Turtles fan, perhaps
21 Israeli airport
22 Did great on, as a test
24 Edgar or Tony
25 Worker's home
26 Foofaraw
27 *The Journey of Natty* ___ (Disney film)
28 Dead duck
29 Ghostly complexions
31 Gondoliers, e.g.
32 Put in a good word for
33 Do in
34 Optimally
37 "Eureka!"
40 Tap troubles
41 Santa's laundry problem
42 Archer with gold-tipped arrows
44 Geiger's first name
45 To the left
46 Carter's middle name
47 Bulldogs backer
48 Varmint
50 Anti–gun control org.
51 Citation, for one
53 Visitor from afar
55 Where Rommel was routed
56 Intended
57 Miles Archer's partner
58 Seine spanners

DOWN

1 Turkey's highest peak
2 Detroit officer of film
3 Oakland's county
4 Sandwich shop choice
5 Ooze
6 Goals of some beachgoers
7 Toward the rudder
8 Out of energy
9 Kenton or Getz
10 *The Joy Luck Club* author
11 Grade
12 Be tabled
13 Alternative to chutes
15 ___ Islands (Antilles group)
20 Seasoned stew
23 Whipped cream helpings
25 Pope's office
28 Lowest among West Point graduates
30 Colleen
31 Nebraska river
33 Abridge
34 Sticks (to)
35 Refrain start
36 News crew's need
37 '82 Hoffman film
38 Rafsanjani, e.g.
39 Flood
41 Like many churches
43 Points of view
45 Bouquet of roses
48 Bloke
49 Interstate exit
52 Subway precursors
54 Composer Delibes

7

by Harold Jones

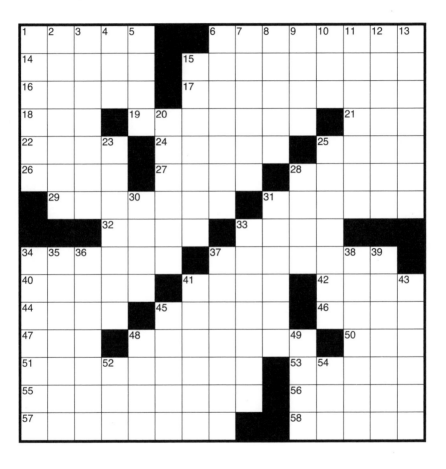

Answer on page 148.

ACROSS

1 Former fireproofing
9 Before '39
15 DMV offering
16 Author Hanff
17 Scatter
18 Beset with criticism
19 Fictional planet
20 College official
22 Agcy. for retirees
23 Shipping hazard
25 White poplar
26 Hill bottoms
27 Become prevalent
29 Arles article
30 Conductor Georg
31 Some cops
33 Legal adverb
34 Newton contemporary
38 Rodeo ropes
39 Ancient Greek region
40 Architect Saarinen
41 Prized possession
42 *Famille* member
46 They may move you
47 *Days of Our Lives* town
49 Two-sided
50 Illustrations
51 Crayon color
53 Phi Bete's pride: Abbr.
54 Yes follower
56 Mental giant
58 Load cargo
59 Got back
60 Hole in your shoe
61 Crabs

DOWN

1 Heated emotions
2 Evening affair
3 Picnic prop
4 The computer world: Abbr.
5 Plan part
6 ___ incognita
7 Italian entrée
8 *1941* director
9 Lunar phenomenon
10 What's left
11 Transportation to Evanston
12 Sneaky sort
13 Popular cordial
14 Connectedness
21 "___ Buttermilk Sky"
24 Limited quantities
26 Presumptuous
28 Like Roseanne's speech
30 Letter flourish
32 ACLU concern
33 Turkey choice
34 Glacial fissure
35 Boisterous humor
36 ___ *County* (Liz Taylor film)
37 Less attractive
41 *The Beggar's Opera* writer
43 Northwest college town
44 Double-edged sword
45 Serengeti sprinters
47 Shipboard shooting
48 Scottish saint
51 ___ Trophy (biennial golf
    tournament)
52 Biblical hunter
55 Th.D.'s specialty
57 Word that starts with an
    apostrophe

8

by Wayne R. Williams

ACROSS

1 Abraham made one
9 Piston packer
15 Wheeler-dealer
16 On duty
17 Put down
18 Not as nice
19 Slugger Slaughter
20 Requisite
22 Watchdog's warning
23 TV room
24 Collate
25 "___ was saying ..."
26 Racer Bobby
30 Barnyard grub
32 Never, in Nuremberg
33 *Northern Exposure* setting
35 Passion
37 Heroine's combination, often
41 Cow catcher
42 Tile mural
43 Christening initials
44 Flat-bottomed boat
46 Fishing line
49 Shoebox letters
50 Prince and March
52 Author Fleming
54 *Delta of Venus* author
55 Some Louvre works
57 Regarding
58 Involve
60 Couldn't take
62 Inscribed stones
63 Gleason epithet
64 Miffed to the max
65 Competitors

DOWN

1 Encrypted
2 First game
3 Capulets' community
4 Deific bowman
5 Emulate Mrs. Mitty
6 ___ impasse
7 Treasury offerings
8 Source of forbidden fruit
9 Specialized cell
10 Served well against
11 Penn or Victoria: Abbr.
12 Rodgers score, with *The*
13 Inside-out position
14 Airedales, e.g.
21 Worries about
27 Heinrich's home
28 Choir members
29 Give, as odds
31 "Splish Splash" singer
34 Mead subject
36 Dash, for one
37 Ocean quality
38 Adopt gradually
39 Sycophant
40 ___-relief
45 St. Moritz shelter
47 Clay victim
48 Beneath the surface
51 Stem's other end
53 Junction points
55 Amnesty International concern
56 Manuscript instruction
57 Four-legged sleuth
59 Draft pick?
61 Musical talent

9

BY RANDOLPH ROSS

ACROSS

1 Common mineral
5 Like a papoose, perhaps
14 Start of a Hammer title
16 Game show consolation prize
17 Singer Marie
18 Woody Allen movie
19 Out-and-out
21 Dazzling effect
22 ___-Turn
23 Brainy?
26 Mideast title
27 Limelike
29 Otoe prey
30 Goldwyn discovery of the '30s
31 Jeff Bridges title role
33 Most old hat
35 Golfer Baker-Finch
36 Cork's loc.
37 Acts the dilettante
41 Piano devices
45 "___ a bad moon rising"
46 Certain inmate
48 Word with turkey or fox
49 PTA setting
50 Rhapsodic
52 Actress Hagen
53 Idle chatter
55 Planting time
57 Eschew roomies
60 Pa Walton portrayer
61 Deviation
62 Nitrite, for one
63 "You betcha!"
64 Pianist Myra

DOWN

1 Ninja Turtles, e.g.
2 Craft on runners
3 Poetic pause
4 Half of A.D.
5 New ___, Connecticut
6 Closet contents
7 False front
8 Formerly, in a sense
9 R.U.R. name
10 Julia Roberts's brother
11 "It doesn't matter now"
12 Makes boil
13 Somewhat aloof
15 1 on the Mohs scale
20 In a polished way
24 Aegean isle
25 Like some prejudiced people
28 Chief's group
30 Was off guard
32 Prefix for function
34 Phonograph part
37 Show off
38 Attribute
39 Isn't bad
40 Gielgud's title
41 Made an edict
42 Knowledgeable
43 Goes around
44 They're long-lasting
47 Stag guest
50 Absorb
51 Wayne's World actor
54 Actress Hatcher
56 Reaction of a sort
58 Sonnyboy
59 What I may mean

10

BY TRIP PAYNE

ACROSS

1 Not great
8 Carries off
15 Checker, perhaps
16 Second solo Atlantic flier
17 Train bridge
18 Archie, to Edith
19 Concession closing
20 Give an address
22 Cow-feteria?
23 Miss Ballou
24 I may follow it
25 Sand toys
27 Solemn sounds
29 Holm et al.
31 Throat germs
32 Kaiser, for one
33 Intense bitterness
35 Some sauces
38 La Douce's namesakes
42 With full knowledge
43 Lorraine's neighbor
44 Berth place
45 Frozen menaces
47 FDR or JFK
48 Mme. of Madrid
49 Bears, to Brutus
50 ___ precedent
51 Word in a Michelangelo
   biography
54 Lacking warmth
56 Land-rich
57 Plant apertures
58 Sibyl was one
59 ___ throw away

DOWN

1 Storms
2 Different spelling
3 Aerobicist, e.g.
4 Stand
5 Formal decision
6 French mathematician
7 Roger the reviewer
8 Museum patrons
9 Moderate
10 Soft & ___
11 Top of the dial
12 ___ day
13 Sapling
14 Stuttgart thoroughfare
21 Praise
24 Matterhorn man
25 SAT instruments
26 Fall bloomers
28 Conductor James
30 Dawson or Deighton
32 Westminster entrants
34 Flat fish
35 Salon preparations
36 Inform
37 Stick anew
39 Mob inductee
40 Transparency material
41 *Año* components
43 Catalysts, for instance
46 Naina's predecessor
49 Nice ones
50 Sapporo sport
52 Coal or wood product
53 Mineralogist's suffix
55 On a streak

11

BY RANDOLPH ROSS

ACROSS

1 Be unmoved
10 Thatcher successor
15 Speaking fees
16 Showing wonder
17 Grad school hurdles
18 Cut partner
19 London's area: Abbr.
20 Ledger term
21 Cathedral officials
22 Perfect grades
24 Strained, old-style
26 *The Missle Crisis* author Abel
27 Cancels out
29 Race reporter of yore
31 Bit of trivia
32 Becomes more abrupt
34 Boris Badenov's boss
36 Grid protection
37 Reverberate
38 Kind of dish
40 Watchdogs, maybe
44 Reaction place
45 *Merry Company* painter
47 Name on a plane
48 Eyes, poetically
50 Greek statesman
52 More than peeved
53 Irving's wife, in the comics
55 Former NFLer
57 Wass or Williams
58 It may be bid
59 Soon
61 Onetime MTV reporter Kurt
62 History class diagrams
63 Wield
64 Education program

DOWN

1 Sports locks
2 Missing, as a coupon
3 France's other name
4 Lon of Cambodia
5 ___ *Scott v. Sandford*
6 Sends, perhaps
7 Graceful horses
8 Prose features
9 Point of some tests
10 DUI fighters
11 Correspond
12 Bridgeport sport
13 Premiere
14 Miracle setting
23 Word often preceding "here"
25 Quaquaversal shapes
28 Booms and gaffs
30 Yammer
33 Adds commas, e.g.
35 Filled pancakes
37 Full range
38 Logical curiosity
39 Righteous Brothers hit
40 Don Johnson ex
41 Roman goddess
42 Less sluggish
43 Superlatively pitiful
44 Setting
46 Chipped flint
49 Utter
51 Appointed to office
54 Mongol tent
56 Inch fractions
60 NCAA rival

12

BY TRIP PAYNE

ACROSS

1 Came of age
8 Chiromancer
15 Say again
16 Property recipient
17 Theater troupes
18 Rummy variety
19 Go up against
20 Opal ending
22 Small change: Abbr.
23 I as in Innsbruck
24 Slips up
25 *Gilligan's Island* star
26 "Take ___ Train"
28 French painter
29 Drunkard
30 Insinuating sneaks
32 Rig workers
33 Addition needs
35 Witchery
38 Encircles
42 Fish-eating fliers
43 Irritated
44 Part of DOS
45 Holiday quaffs
46 *Mr. Mom* name
47 Kyushu volcano
48 Ecol. org.
49 Pop song section
51 Ran like madras
52 Friz Freleng feature
54 Like loyal fans
56 Score direction
57 *Phormio* playwright
58 Oracle
59 Means of access

DOWN

1 Square pegs
2 Traveling case
3 Eli, to Samuel
4 Argue for
5 *Norma* ___
6 To be, in Toulouse
7 Lunch counter displays
8 Rabbits, to greyhounds
9 Sues and Shepard
10 Dryer trappings
11 ___ *culpa*
12 Poet's perception
13 Pioneer, perhaps
14 Affectionate critics
21 Puzzling phenomenon?
25 *The Planets* composer et al.
27 Orange mismatches
28 Endangered antelopes
29 Turner of rock
31 Right-angle shapes
32 Double curve
34 Wet fields
35 Iroquois Confederacy
   members
36 Barbecue fuel
37 Fighting words
39 Transparent substance
40 Pith
41 Stuffs oneself
43 Fishing nets
46 Harness races
49 It may be picked
50 Hagman costar
51 Rabbit's title
53 Old salt
55 Food scrap

13

by Wayne R. Williams

ACROSS

1 Grouse, e.g.
9 Track sounds
14 Handel specialty
15 Nickname of '40s All-Star Harry Brecheen
16 Hedonistic
17 Spanish muralist
18 Holden's last film
19 Holds rapt
21 Cartographer's abbr.
22 Portuguese plaudits
24 Jetson kid
25 James Stewart thriller
26 Thurmond and Archibald
28 Tokyo's former name
29 Tropical palm
30 Critic Gene's family
32 Wine descriptor
33 Defeats in bridge
34 Stop, as a game
35 Loses freshness
38 Hair apparent?
41 Confess
42 Campaigner, for short
43 Tray contents
45 Slacks specification
46 Spite, so to speak
48 Bodybuilder's concern
49 Montgomery sch.
50 Hits the sack
52 Director Howard
53 Four-legged shepherd
55 Swamp plants
57 Sends by computer
58 *Oklahoma!* role
59 Put in play
60 It's unresolved

DOWN

1 Sponsored child
2 Colorful rings
3 Trouper's bad luck word
4 SFO abbr.
5 Indicate by signs
6 Castle Walk proponent
7 Girls' curls
8 Doddering ones
9 X X X
10 *My Name Is Asher* ___
11 They're spotted in Mexico
12 Fort wall
13 Like the minuet
15 Certain domino
20 Sloppy stuff
23 Shell-less mollusk
25 Practical sort
27 "Silent Night" word
29 Spewack of Broadway
31 "___ Magic"
32 Go off course
34 Grand Canyon carver
35 Cheers up
36 Pair
37 Eclipse type
38 Pylon-shaped
39 Woman in a revue
40 *Queens Logic* star
42 Creature comfort?
44 Had a hunch
46 Volvo parts?
47 Copycat's phrase
50 Fire up
51 B&O stops
54 One of Ingmar's favorite actresses
56 *Wheel of Fortune* buy

14

by Trip Payne

ACROSS

1 Name of five Spanish kings
7 Handel work based on biblical stories
14 Maigret's creator
15 Hardly mature
16 Dream states
17 Warrants
18 Betting setting
19 Elizabeth II, to Edward VIII
21 Scoundrel
22 G.P.'s gp.
23 Ride, in a way
25 Sonora snapshot
26 Father figure
28 Cannoneer, at times
29 More underhanded
30 At ___ (speechless)
31 Mercury, for one
33 Part with
35 Largest terrier
39 Urban districts
40 Insult
41 Field of knowledge
42 Fancy flapjacks
43 Victrola developer
44 Interstate sign
45 Comic strip waif
46 Bed support
47 Slippery
49 Religious recluse
52 Throws out
53 Hallowed halls
54 Lawn equipment
55 Rich desserts

DOWN

1 *Backdraft* character
2 Stem (from)
3 Founder of Big Dog Productions
4 Small business mag
5 "Eldorado" writer
6 Involves in intrigue
7 Address
8 Not a heavy weight
9 ___ majesty (high crime)
10 Tulsa sch.
11 Magician's secret
12 Tallow derivatives
13 Trojan War name
14 Watch holders
20 Built up
23 Cheapskates
24 Contract provision
25 Some seaways: Var.
27 Best Western alternative
28 Band on the run
30 Consent
32 Most brisk
33 Universally liked one?
34 Take for granted
36 Carrier of a sort
37 Fixes
38 Mom's kin
39 Puts up
40 *Gunsmoke* star
42 Minimum charge
45 Swan, e.g.
46 Struck down, old-style
48 Grassy surface
50 Greek letter
51 Miscalculate

15

BY RANDOLPH ROSS

ACROSS

1 Brunch selection
10 Orbit point
15 Smithsonian stuff
16 Word on a tractor
17 Loverboys
18 Artistic style
19 Some collars
20 "Outer" word form
21 Lustrous material
22 Double-decker checker
23 Act I word
25 Diminished by
26 Former card-issuing org.
27 Togged out
29 Small beef
30 Ran quickly
31 Cut free
33 Yevtushenko poem
36 House
37 Los ___, New Mexico
38 Light racing boat
39 Singer Ocasek
40 Adds up
42 Cable overseers: Abbr.
45 Puts on the line
47 City on the Rhone
48 *How Green Was My Valley* material
49 Wind: Prefix
51 Took in
52 Mystic force
53 Less everyday
54 Imitates Robinson
56 Ready to joust
57 Nebraska residents, e.g.
58 Holds, as a car
59 Paul McCartney tune

DOWN

1 Diacritical marks
2 Classic instruments
3 Pions and kaons
4 Big ape
5 Time segs.
6 *Foucault's Pendulum* author
7 Pale purple
8 Put through
9 Tried some of
10 Take ___ (swim)
11 Sostenuto, for one
12 School catcher
13 Burr role
14 About four months
23 Large land mass
24 Frat hopefuls
27 ___ reckoning
28 Comes off in sheets
30 Presidential pooch
32 Presidential nickname
33 Bush and Rush
34 Drive away
35 Pathogens, often
36 Multi-layered
38 Seedless grape
41 For nothing
42 Is compelling
43 Image maker
44 Stylish
46 Trout cousin
48 Onetime penny purchase
50 Crumbs and such
52 Japanese writing system
55 Article written by Goethe

16

BY TRIP PAYNE

ACROSS

1 Rhode Island nickname
11 Hines specialty
14 Nine-time Wimbledon singles champ
16 The Buckeyes
17 Citrine coolers
18 Durocher, familiarly
19 Bring to naught
20 Magic stick
21 Think tank output
23 Film holder
24 Robert's daughter on *Father Knows Best*
26 Karate skill level
29 Cariou of *Sweeney Todd* on Broadway
30 Erstwhile auto
33 Printer's proof
35 Long time: Abbr.
36 Jerk's locale
37 Worthless talk
38 Martian feature
40 European car
41 Track alternative
44 Senior member
45 Styling job
46 It's refined
47 Mouse-o-phobe's cry
48 *A Civil Tongue* author
50 "This can't be!"
54 Lamb Chop's handler
56 Wherein you'll see the light
59 Tooth's partner
60 Finless fish
61 Card game
64 Entirely
65 African high spot
66 Get a load of
67 Breathed colleague

DOWN

1 "Maladies are taxes ___ joys": Byron
2 Judy of *Laugh-In*
3 Get around
4 Army leader
5 Harper
6 Internalize anger
7 Mia Farrow's sister
8 *The Heart Is* ___ *Hunter*
9 Rug rat
10 Spacewalk, to NASA
11 Range of variation
12 See 25-Down
13 Little boxers
15 A-apple link
22 Arcade game
25 With 12-Down, Gunther book
27 Uris hero
28 "... ___ at the inn"
31 Young of *The Boost*
32 Wise, man
33 Hitchcock thriller
34 Ever
37 Short flight
39 Iowa college
42 Vocal filler
43 Bhutto of Pakistan
49 Lighter part
51 Mirthful sounds
52 "Soup"
53 Game show announcer Johnny
54 Black and Red, but not Green
55 Beatles #1 tune
57 "For shame!"
58 Thunderous sound
62 Horse and carriage
63 One ___ million

17

BY MATT GAFFNEY

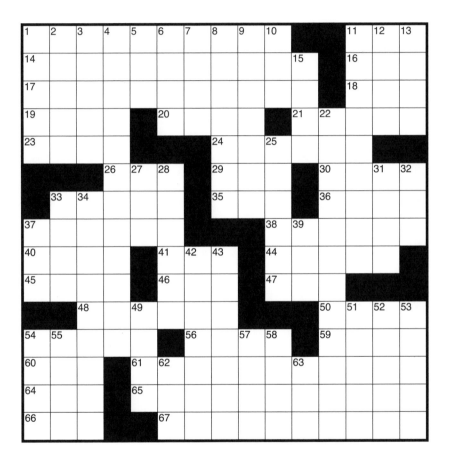

Answer on page 156.

ACROSS

1 This
10 Siberian citizen
15 Atticus's creator
16 Steal the scene
17 Garden flower
18 '92 sitcom
19 Rubber-stamp word
20 Filmdom's "Danielle" et al.
22 Cal. page
23 Two of Henry's six
25 Eurasian bird
26 Tall antenna
27 Ascertain
28 Borg and Edberg
30 Kind of clef
31 Like ___ (candidly)
32 Less used, perhaps
34 Prendergast's school
37 Ebert and others
38 Proof subject, in math
40 Salon items
41 Intrude, with "in"
42 Sunshades
44 Talk excessively
47 Thirteen popes
48 City near Turin
49 Former Intellivision rival
51 *The Book of* ___ (Denzel Washington film)
52 Buffet heater
54 Mass ending
55 *Famille* member
57 Quarter-mile sport
59 Minimal change
60 '80s sports star
61 Sports basket
62 S-shaped sofa

DOWN

1 Bar order
2 Punk singer Joey
3 Succulent plant
4 Falcon hunter
5 Wave and curl
6 Sealed order
7 Some ointments
8 Let
9 Coveted after
10 Shackelford and Knight
11 "Botch-___"
12 Wasn't straight
13 Witness bearer
14 Energy sources
21 Guarantor
24 Spectral type
26 Houston and Biondi
29 Port holder
31 Religious symbols
33 Catsup alternative
34 Muscular and fit
35 Oxford insert
36 Thelma and Louise
39 Botch the galleys
40 Assailing
43 Made an effort
44 Leslie Caron type
45 Historian Hannah
46 Personal ad beginning
50 Score notation
52 ___ good example
53 Alençon's department
56 Big bang cause
58 Like

18

BY TRIP PAYNE

ACROSS

1 *Honeymoon in Vegas* star
5 Rocket launcher
9 "... lamb was ___ go"
11 Tasmanian capital
13 Certain Mexican
14 Code of silence
15 Bad talk
16 Spreading out for drying
18 Meyers and Onassis
19 Bard's black
21 "Ignorance ___ excuse"
22 Copy
24 Sound of discomfort
25 Issue side
26 Constitutional guarantee
29 Park Service employees
30 Psalms phrase
36 Loved ones
37 Wish undone
38 Game-catching device
39 Icicle holder
40 Gehrig replaced him
41 CCIII tripled
42 Tinny
44 Claret, e.g.
47 Secret stuff
48 May et al.
49 Unsaturated organic chemical
50 Pizzeria pieces
51 *Not Without My Daughter* locale
52 Miss America accessory

DOWN

1 Librarian, at times
2 Atmospheric word form
3 *Pictures ___ Exhibition*
4 Shapeless
5 Name: Latin
6 Still sleeping
7 Lunch order
8 Creative type
9 Not as pleasant
10 Green
11 Just out
12 Astringent acid
13 Devour, with "down"
17 Mild oath
20 Give confidence to
23 Rank sensations
25 ___-ski
27 "It must be him ___ shall die"
28 Date
30 February 13th, e.g.
31 ___ a pin
32 Imported cheese
33 Lake Michigan city
34 Threesomes
35 Is bewitching
40 Southwestern tree
43 First capital of Japan
45 Scarlett's daughter in *Scarlett*
46 Honoree's place

19

BY RANDOLPH ROSS

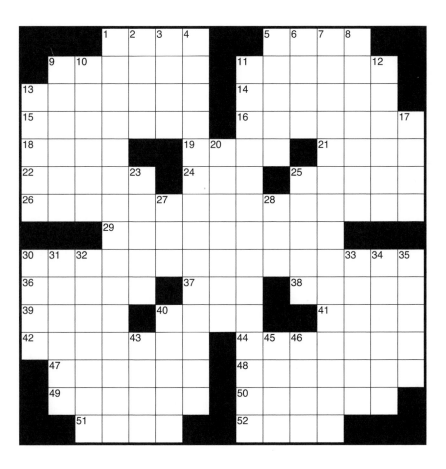

ACROSS

1 Henry Morgan was one
7 Slanders
15 Mite family
16 Cart crossbar
17 Hoisting need?
18 *The Guns of Navarone* actress
19 Imitate Cicero
20 The opposition
21 Tender an offer
22 Into view
23 Ridley Scott film
24 "Toodles!"
25 Chips and such
28 "Totally bogus," e.g.
29 Nature lovers
30 Tester output
31 Pupils' spots
32 "Hang on a minute!"
33 Tide rival
35 Connick and Crosby
39 Windblown silt
40 Diamond position
41 *Picnic* man
42 Follow Yamaguchi
43 Verb ending
44 Fi preceder
45 Book part
46 ___ *millésime* (vintage year)
48 Utterly uncivilized
50 Maia or Electra
51 Radio serial sponsor
52 Paste stuff
53 Some savings
54 Makes up

DOWN

1 Young Ute
2 Tobogganing slides
3 Rapper's sound
4 It's often smelled
5 Jade
6 Baseball Hall of Famer Roush
7 Bathhouses
8 Went off
9 Done in
10 Fiddle (with)
11 "You get the idea": Abbr.
12 Fine horse
13 Trusting
14 Tar
20 Word in a Fugard title
23 Half an ad?
24 Makes presentable
26 Beaufort or Beaumont
27 *Flowers for Algernon* author
28 Get outta there
30 Vacation spot
32 Put down
33 Like some lenses
34 Flights of a sort
35 Raffle tickets
36 Harrovian's rival
37 Optimistic
38 Swimmers' wear
39 Prince Henry's capital
40 Killy's skill
42 Small spray
45 Fill to the brim
46 Like crazy
47 *Nautilus* name
49 Ham alternative
50 Elem. gp.

20

BY TRIP PAYNE

ACROSS

1 Balance indicator
10 Old Italian bread
14 Sight from Cairo
15 Ur's area
16 Run down
17 Sinclair character
18 Indonesia divisions
19 Ted Danson role
21 Potsdam preposition
22 Skip a round
23 Some gridders: Abbr.
24 Fibber McGee's closet, e.g.
25 Farmers, often
26 With no delay
27 *Wagon Train* star
28 Put on
29 Starts growing
33 Braced (oneself)
35 Minuscule
36 Dudweiler's location
37 Compass dirs.
38 Old World ducks
40 It's often gathered
44 Watch display, for short
45 Young lions
46 Clear conclusion
47 Marlee Matlin, for one
49 "Dialogues" author
50 Spock, but not Kirk
51 Religious freethinker
53 Halfhearted
54 Wave of a sort
55 *Paradise Lost* setting
56 Close colleagues

DOWN

1 Volatile element
2 Pyramus's love
3 Places for rolling?
4 Bar-crawlers
5 Important times
6 Former Russian space station
7 Means of escape
8 Canceled out
9 Aftershock, for example
10 Break in the action
11 Hall of Famer
12 Get back into battle
13 Brought in
15 Pants part
20 Frat letters
22 Used up
26 *Sacrée* woman: Abbr.
27 Get for oneself
28 Soap opera: Abbr.
29 Star-shaped
30 Drew, in a way
31 Organ tube
32 Switch positions
33 Was published
34 *Pravda* source
36 Corrosive acid
38 ___ Na Na
39 One of the Gorgons
40 Carpenter's co-diner
41 Put ___ (be haughty)
42 From C to C
43 Director Sergio et al.
45 Make (one's way)
48 Hold back
49 Clip
52 ___ Borch (Dutch painter)

21

BY TRIP PAYNE

ACROSS

1 Parking lot feature
10 WWII fliers
13 Newark native
14 Authors Godwin and Sheehy
16 Suited for singing
17 Stop at the Sorbonne
18 Thorny quality
19 "___ cockhorse to Banbury Cross"
20 IV × CCLI
21 Cardinal insignia
22 Comics GI
24 Nautical boom
26 Henry ___ Commager
28 Palmer's peg
29 Character actor Jack
31 Tavern patrons
33 Business cycle component
36 Hardly invigorating
39 Dupe
42 Campus in Tulsa, OK
43 Battleground of 1862
46 Cup lip
48 Selling for
50 O.T. book
52 Poli follower
53 ___ level (legit)
54 Ready to go again
57 Bucks, but not dollars
58 Bringing to life
59 Cast off from the body
60 Receptivity
61 Palindromic preposition
62 Nightmarish address

DOWN

1 Earthshaking events
2 Pastoral instrument
3 Summery
4 Cornwallis's alma mater
5 France's patron
6 Small geese
7 Remove a safety strap
8 *Alice*'s restaurant
9 Dry cleaner employees
10 "___ hell": Sherman
11 Broadcast time
12 Con man
14 *The ___ Allah* (Dietrich film)
15 Poker parameters
23 *Et ___*
25 Unusual
27 Ford family member
30 Most muddled
32 Turner seen on TV?
34 James Woods role
35 Leave home, in a way
36 Ahead
37 When forging started
38 Range robber
40 Rain ___
41 Dual carriageway user's need
44 Captured, perhaps
45 Mercury's alias
47 Small salami
49 This and that
51 *Damn Yankees* tune
55 Organic compound
56 Name over the title

22

BY RANDOLPH ROSS

Answer on page 154.

ACROSS

1 Hard finish
9 They lead charmed lives
15 Parting word
16 Get one's bearings
17 Menu phrase
18 Counteract
19 Bastille Day time
20 Felt nostalgia for
22 Encouraging words
23 Felt
25 ___ thought (daydreaming)
27 Expecting
30 Small degree
32 Bouquets
35 On the fringe
36 "___ Got a Crush on You"
37 Jones of the sea
38 Hatcher and Copley
39 Just swell
40 Soul, to Sartre
41 Plaster of Paris
42 ___-face (affectionate)
43 Crosby's *Star Trek* role
44 Allowing for mistakes
46 Ancient Greek coin
48 Descriptive history
52 Scrutinize
53 Emulates Electra
56 Pull down
57 Group of six
59 End, to a center
61 Kind of show
62 Earnest attempt
63 Ditch
64 *Bad Boys* star

DOWN

1 Farm enclosures
2 Italian noble
3 German flowers
4 *Fables in Slang* author
5 Finger pointers
6 Next to
7 Lorelei Lee's creator
8 Ages and ages
9 Gives tacit approval to
10 Vein contents
11 Bunker, for one
12 Truths
13 Church areas
14 Holy women: Abbr.
21 High spirits
24 Full of life
26 Bering, for example: Abbr.
28 Loses amateur status
29 White hat wearer
31 Say it isn't so
32 Singer with Krupa
33 Certain Syrian
34 Asks too much of
38 Run-down apartment
39 Hot spot
41 "Scram, varmint!"
42 Uncles and nephews
45 Second-largest nation
47 Make ___ for oneself
49 Yucca's family
50 Admit
51 After part
52 Ready for a hike
54 Colorado Indians
55 Painter Magritte
58 Org. founded in 1890
60 Road rally need

23

BY TRIP PAYNE

ACROSS

1 Tousling
8 Give a frisking
14 Set for young builders
15 Rider's charge
16 Siberian borderer
17 Mole, e.g.
18 Charisma
20 It hangs by the neck
21 "Swing and Sway" Kaye
22 Brazilian Indian
23 Some bridge players
26 Teddy's Italian namesake
27 Take to one's heels
29 Iacocca's successor at Chrysler
31 Spelling groups?
32 Sweepstakes decider
35 Common Christie clue
36 Deals (out)
37 Tackle box contents
38 ___ Xing (street sign)
39 Non-italic type
43 Compass pt.
44 *Network* Oscar winner
46 In the past
47 Preview promise
52 ___ fashion (trend follower)
53 Polonius's daughter
54 Most snaky
55 Meager
56 Sailor's protector
57 Shot source

DOWN

1 *Kiss* ___
2 Astronomer's Muse
3 *Fish* and *CHiPs*
4 Con man's forte
5 "___ Miracle" (Manilow tune)
6 Songs in the snow
7 Chemist's unit
8 Optimistic
9 Latin verb
10 Throw ___ (rage)
11 Hams, e.g.
12 Reaching a peak
13 Herman's backup
15 Battleship's nickname
19 Constitutional postscript
24 Uptight
25 Javanese carriages
27 Turn down
28 Dispatch boat
30 Cargo unit
31 Scanning acronym
32 Small circle
33 Terrier type
34 Group founded in 1864
35 Tickles pink
38 Physicist Henri
40 Remit
41 Have ___ concern (conduct business)
42 Minority
44 Dom DeLuise movie
45 Grumpy's brother
48 Like Hannibal Lecter
49 Judge
50 Cook a bit too well
51 Polo of *Meet the Parents*

24

BY ALICE LONG

ACROSS

1 Centerfold intrusion
7 Zealot
14 Radioactive thorium
15 Small-minded
16 Byrds tune
18 "Make ___ double!"
19 Engaged in a bit of legerdemain
20 Heros
21 Lady of Las Vegas?
23 Come back
24 Card game
25 First sign of spring
27 Reggae's roots
28 Sacrifice site
30 Mirrored word in *The Shining*
32 Where a leg may be
34 Chordettes tune
36 Hunt eels
38 Cicero or Cato
42 Pickle
43 ___ *Boot* ('81 film)
45 Newsperson Sawyer
46 Track unit
47 Virgil described its eruption
49 Floored it
50 Lively, in mus.
52 Idealistic
54 Prefix for cure
55 Marvelettes tune
58 Arbors
59 Aaron Burr's birthplace
60 Show biz autobio
61 Some PBS funding

DOWN

1 Analogous
2 Dungeon doings
3 Heartburn aid
4 Singer Zadora
5 Coffee additive
6 Put a stop to
7 Rough translation of "Tierra del Fuego"
8 Bitterish
9 Palindromic nickname
10 Vote carriers
11 Uproars
12 "Picture yourself ___ on a river ..."
13 Network naysayer
15 Peter et al.
17 Corrida cries
22 *Muppet Show* host
26 Voltage jump
28 "Pick ___, any ..."
29 Maui verandas
31 Food seasoning, for short
33 Latin 101 verb
35 City official
36 Spider-Man's co-creator
37 ___ bones (early calculator)
39 Surveyor's assistant
40 Uninterrupted
41 Enters losses
42 Comic White
44 Pre-Velcro item
47 Journalist ___ Rogers St. Johns
48 In the thick of
51 Epiphany arrivals
53 River of north France
56 Part of SPCA
57 Erstwhile American rival

25

BY ALICE LONG

ACROSS

1 Ming the Merciless or Nero
7 Jacket fasteners
14 Optics adjective
15 Elevate
16 Whistle-blower
17 Butcher
18 GNP or RBI
19 Service response
21 Express
22 Diet lunches
25 Bring to a boil?
26 Honor with insults
27 Norton's office?
31 Characters in *The Odyssey*
33 Sky screamer, once
35 It's held by Swiss banks
36 Colonel's command
37 In neutral
39 Caterpillar construction
40 Bracketed word
43 Crop plane
44 Adlai's partner
46 Milky Way dazzlers
48 British suffix
49 Policemen, at times
52 D.C. lobbyer
55 Good place to have a cow?
56 Sponsorship
57 Conscience-stricken
59 Rotten egg, perhaps?
61 Angora relative
62 Approaches
63 Had ambitions
64 French legislatures

DOWN

1 Third degrees, perhaps
2 Packaging
3 Rabbit tails
4 Ballet step
5 Takes too much
6 Singer Stratas
7 Commotions
8 *Robin Hood*, for one
9 Upright relatives
10 *Bugsy* prop
11 Like a wet noodle
12 Genesis redhead
13 Delighted
14 Dress down
20 Itar-___ (news agency)
23 Ages
24 Navy divers
28 Biding one's time
29 Lily Tomlin character et al.
30 Goes back
32 Smee and Starbuck
34 Krakatoa phenomenon
38 Where to see a second helping
41 Began hostilities
42 Mixed
45 Kind of squash or sausage
47 Some strings
50 Ebbets Field shortstop
51 Empedocles's last stand?
52 "*¿Qué* ___?"
53 Garage sale caveat
54 Bloke
58 Corday's confidant
60 Boxer's title, for short

26

BY RANDOLPH ROSS

ACROSS

1 Killer ending
5 Eucharistic vestment
12 Broods
14 At rest, maybe
15 Last words at Wimbledon
17 First name in fashion
18 Furnishings
19 Round (out)
20 Mixed bags
22 One of the lower forty
23 "If You Go Away" composer
24 Mario's maker
26 "It's ___-pipe cinch"
28 Vb. type
29 Flaky
31 Raggedy name
32 Inflatable item?
33 Farm machines
35 Infield stats: Abbr.
38 Buckeye coll.
40 Wild and white
41 Robert Morse role
42 Layette fasteners
44 "I'd be glad to!"
46 Norman city
47 MIT grad
49 It won't hold water
50 "___ for apple"
51 Enjoy
53 Tease a tad
54 Impossible retrieval
58 Working for peanuts
59 Tanker taboos
60 Gallo and Worrell
61 Beth preceder

DOWN

1 Arrive
2 "___ a Feeling" (*Let It Be* song)
3 Plaines preceder
4 Checked out
5 Not worth mentioning
6 Singer McArdle
7 Grunt grounds
8 O.T. book
9 Prokofiev piece
10 Was short
11 One of the Kennedys
12 Avon's business?
13 More reliable
15 Spielberg character
16 Consistent with
21 Closes the deal
23 Big bonger
25 Social register word
27 *Rawhide* props
30 Social requirements
34 CSA fighter
36 Composer André's family
37 French FBI
39 Japanese honorific
42 Fleet fellow
43 Be of a mind (to)
45 Famed footballer Y.A.
46 Sweater stitch
48 Aromatic ointments
52 Mama's boy?
55 Unlock, to Arnold
56 ___ *Rheingold*
57 Part of RSVP

27

by Randolph Ross

ACROSS

1 Party decoration
9 Mary Janes, e.g.
14 Fracture type
15 They're found on some sleeves
17 Chess stages
18 Guarantee
19 Bass, for one
20 Sea nymphs
22 Math abbr.
23 Fissures
25 Handed out
26 Diving position
27 Genesis name
28 Auel character
29 Mosquito or mad dog
30 Implant anew
32 Angry Airedales
34 Streisand film
36 Belligerent deity
37 Purple-berry tree
41 Jousting needs
45 *Hamlet* prop
46 Fair, briefly
48 Iberian river
49 Mai ___ (cocktails)
50 Not quite never
51 Olivia's *Captain Blood* costar
52 "Life ___ Highway" ('92 song)
53 Satellite dish alternative
55 Oklahoma city
56 Started from scratch
58 In serial form
60 Verdi opera
61 News story starter
62 ___ example
63 Huskies

DOWN

1 *The Divorcee* Oscar winner
2 Beachgoer's concern
3 ___ a fall (invite trouble)
4 Dyne-centimeter
5 Ladd and Bates
6 Shields or Yarnell
7 Vim and vigor
8 Closes back up
9 Hades inhabitant
10 English pianist
11 PAU outgrowth
12 Obviously learned
13 Picket
16 Cuts
21 Donald's first ex
24 '92 primary candidate
26 Light lager
28 Boy or girl lead-in
29 La ___ Tar Pits
31 Inclusive pronoun
33 Woody's son
35 Really tired
37 *Mad* specialty
38 Delete key ancestors
39 She handed Theseus a line
40 Tops
42 Trucker's need
43 Glacial activity
44 Gives comfort
47 Foreign correspondent
50 ___ a million
51 Greased the wheels
53 Leo's heroine
54 Evening, in ads
57 Mill grist
59 No longer fresh

28

BY TRIP PAYNE

ACROSS

1 Admit
8 Eerie atmospheres
15 Museum display
16 Taking a sabbatical
17 Martian, in movies
18 Waned, with "out"
19 ___ Dee River
20 Sign of rank
22 Green Mountain Boy ___ Allen
23 He was in tents
25 Impressed immensely
26 Act as usher
27 Less loopy
29 Low
30 Fright site?
31 "... the ___ the earth"
33 Called to court
35 Ecclesiastical headdress
37 Put on a coat
38 Tailed
41 Like a lullaby
44 Merchandise
45 U.S. pres., e.g.
47 Makes argyles
48 Pretension
49 ___ Hashanah
50 Punkie or midge
51 Soft & ___ (deodorant)
52 Radio pioneer
55 Drop a brick
56 Classy crystal?
58 Lasagna ingredient
60 Heir
61 With vigilance
62 Put up
63 Tenants

DOWN

1 Tissue type
2 Pass protector
3 Sinatra song
4 ___ pro nobis
5 Cotton balls
6 "___ a man with ..."
7 South African shrub
8 Finished one's business
9 "You're All ___ to Get By"
10 Airplane gauge rdgs.
11 Date regularly
12 '38 title role for Norma Shearer
13 Dean's list determinant
14 Calmed down
21 ___ Monty's Double
24 Crashes permanently?
26 Biblical punishment
28 Sunday paper sections
30 Smile of the smug
32 Slim pickings
34 Meadow remark
36 On tape
38 Wrap up, as a baby
39 More frightful
40 Netflix mailing
42 Tap on the shoulder, maybe
43 Little lost dogies
46 Like a cantata
49 Shillong sovereign
52 Stanton colleague
53 Nelson's river
54 Pushcart purchases
57 Bub
59 Where to find M.D.'s and R.N.'s

29

BY RANDOLPH ROSS

ACROSS

1 Doesn't rush
9 "Oh, is that ___?"
14 Having 1,001 uses
15 A Prentiss
16 Irish Protestants
17 "Norwegian Wood" instrument
18 *Drop Dead Fred* actress
19 *Dating Game* players
21 Son of Hera
22 Taxi features
23 Bush's former agcy.
24 The Mormons, for short
25 Soft touch
26 ___ Webster (Twain's frog)
27 Kramden's collection
28 Henchmen
29 Joan of Arc, for one
31 Jordan score
33 Cocktail garnishes
34 *La vita nuova* author
35 Hand or foot
36 Discuss at length
38 Baseball execs
41 CCXXX × V
42 Stand for
43 Mine transport
44 Onetime Plymouth model
46 Chicago landmark
47 Beelike
48 Stunt man, e.g.
50 Runs wild
51 Revision
52 Start of an Austen title
53 Neighborhood market?

DOWN

1 Poet ___ Manley Hopkins
2 Gets on the stump
3 They did the lord's work
4 Isn't firm
5 Beatified *femme*, for short
6 More like contortionists
7 Some salts
8 Handy man of TV?
9 Basilica parts
10 Refuse to work
11 Presidential procession
12 Woody instrument
13 Foot bones
14 Uttered
20 *Another 48 ___*
22 It's "a grand old name"
25 "Memory" musical
26 Zuider Zee sight
27 Stay awake nights
28 Concerning
29 Thanksgiving dish
30 "Thanks ___!"
31 Good conversationalist
32 Way into the pot
33 Some vertebrae
34 Lifelike display
36 Alt. sheepskin
37 Sometime
38 Driveway material
39 Seascape
40 Silvery fish
42 Muddleheaded
43 Dissertation topic
45 Chemical containers
46 Advantage
49 Wrap up

30

BY TRIP PAYNE

ACROSS

1 Baklava and barquette
9 *21 Jump Street* star
13 Running the show
14 Ballerina Karsavina
16 Aquarium process
17 Corresponds
18 Face lifts?
19 Clean as a whistle
21 Elbow-bender
22 Apparel
23 Numbered hwy.
24 Tolkien creatures
25 Cook for a crowd
26 Trunk feature
27 ___ gestae
28 Convention announcements
30 Hubbub
31 Using a blunt instrument
34 Violin part
37 Klutz's cry
38 Made ___ of oneself
39 ___ colada
40 Lieut.'s "alma mater"
41 Salon supplies
42 1972 agreement
43 Greta Garbo role
46 *Call Me Madam* composer
47 Often-abbreviated phrase
48 Tongue tier?
50 Spoiled
51 Prom date
52 Classic cars
53 Atomizers

DOWN

1 Coin of Cairo
2 Showy flower
3 Where to find lines
4 Greek philosopher
5 Star giver
6 Pupil's locale
7 It's inflatable
8 Media extremists
9 Blowgun missile
10 Pianist Gilels
11 Coaching legend Joe
12 Director Sturges
14 *The Man With* ___
15 Sometimes they're frozen
20 *What's New, Pussycat?* actress
22 Con man, in Cambridge
25 "What's that?"
26 Folks
28 Eggy drink
29 Outfit, with "up"
30 LP replacements
31 Baby follower
32 Boundary tracer
33 Northern New York
34 Act like Attila
35 Temptress
36 Reverse dives
39 Linked bet
42 "I've Just ___ Face" (Beatles tune)
44 Clarinet category
45 Loses no time
46 Transvaal resident
49 With it

31

BY RANDOLPH ROSS

ACROSS

1 Bodybuilder's pride
6 Paper tiger of a sort
15 ___ barrel (helpless)
16 2/2 time
17 Former NFLer Andre
18 Held back
19 Foot part
21 Bearing
22 NSA or BSA
23 Former cable award
24 Former Afghan title
26 Fashion designer Gernreich
27 General vicinity
30 Aluminum boat
31 Square one
32 '87 Pulitzer-winning play
33 CCLXVII × VI
35 *Ciel* dwellers
36 It's shaken for sound
37 Prize money
39 ___ *des Beaux-Arts*
40 Ulna supports
43 AAA handouts
44 Words with line or hint
45 First word on *Monty Python*
47 Supporting
48 Meets a bet
49 Volkswagen model
52 Grant/Loren comedy
55 Stage star Janis
56 Among other things
57 Inundate
58 Whoopi Goldberg movie
59 Martinelli and Lanchester

DOWN

1 *Andrea* ___
2 Show clearly
3 Take away from
4 Harness race
5 Reasonable
6 Italian isle: Abbr.
7 Name of 14 popes
8 Caine character et al.
9 Less typical
10 *Israel in the World* author
11 Dernier ___
12 Swear off
13 Carries too far
14 Some women's shoes
20 Pre-1935 country
25 Comic trio member
26 Meanders
28 Word in liner notes
29 How some foods are packed
30 Perfume
32 Turn-of-the-century soprano
33 Salad ingredient
34 Permanent truants
36 Ruined African city
37 Dull
38 Base man
40 Colorful ring
41 Shinbones
42 Loss of reputation
44 Keep out
46 Arthur Murray lessons
48 Gobi-like
50 Statue site
51 Act like a baby
53 Circle
54 Use a shuttle

32

BY TRIP PAYNE

ACROSS

1 Tamper with
7 Beech Nut competitor
13 Go astray
14 Dolled up
16 Four-term first lady
17 Early sitcom surname
18 Geom. figure
19 Pointillism founder
21 ___ de grâce
22 Gulf state
24 On the tight side
25 Tennis tie
26 Austerity
28 Strike down
30 Thrice, to a pharmacist
31 Audiophile's purchase
33 Breathing devices
35 Goldbricks
37 California island
40 Cocktail choice
44 Capp and Capone
45 Tall stories?
47 Violinist Zimbalist
48 À la King?
50 Goes to pieces
52 Luce publication
53 Made tracks
54 Miles and Brightman
56 Canasta cousin
57 Unpaid landlord, eventually
59 Onetime Rooney colleague
61 Elaborate verse forms
62 Sphinxes
63 Drunk as a skunk
64 Respectful response

DOWN

1 Draw boundaries
2 Excess
3 NSA creation
4 Doe and fawn
5 Oklahoma tribe
6 TV Land fare, often
7 Auto protection
8 Rephrase, perhaps
9 Scheherazade subject
10 Prepare for a blow
11 On the way
12 Weight-watcher
13 Interior designs
15 Drug addicts
20 Pensive person
23 Marilyn, originally
25 Hon
27 In fact
29 Sci-fi classic
32 Gallimaufry
34 Lucky Strike initialism
36 Invisible light
37 Shudra and Vaisya
38 Bays and booths
39 Dictatorial
41 Paper work
42 Educational meeting
43 Peace offering
46 Contrived
49 Verso's opposite
51 Ladd role
54 Loudness measure
55 Hindu honorifics
58 Tole material
60 T-shirt sizes: Abbr.

33

BY RANDOLPH ROSS

ACROSS

1 Inns of Court member
10 ___ *dixit*
14 Any
15 "O Tannenbaum," e.g.
16 What cell phones lack
17 Anoint
18 Runner Zátopek
19 Biology class subject
21 MC's need
22 *Come September* star
24 Cheer up
25 Felix Silla role
26 Light bedstead
28 Perfect things
29 Canal zone?
30 More ghoulish
33 Stammering sounds
34 The Thompson Twins, for one
35 Forms of genes
37 *Panama Hattie* actress
39 Dressed
40 Belli or Bailey: Abbr.
42 Candy brand
43 ___ Tafari
44 Morgan marking
45 Crushed
46 Tag people
47 Late wake-up call
49 Symbolic representation
53 Main
54 Shook up
56 Function of sorts
57 Tasteless
59 Cigar type
61 Fictional terrier et al.
62 *Havana* actor
63 Cardinal's residence
64 Ore-Ida products

DOWN

1 Portended
2 Jungian term
3 Publicize again
4 Was carefree
5 Old NYC subway line
6 Metropolitan problem
7 Musically traditional
8 Recluse
9 Cuts again
10 Famous Fleming
11 Opening nights
12 Patience, e.g.
13 Thomson discovery
15 Author Herb and family
20 Some muscles
23 Coward of fame
27 Bore the expense
30 Vestment official
31 Uncomfortable
32 Outstanding sorts
34 Ship of ___ (camel)
36 Don't draw
38 Wild spree
41 Lilting sound
44 Collar needs
48 ___ Work
50 Silvers role
51 Dark
52 Penn and Young
55 Esbjerg resident
58 Herriman feline
60 Smoke solids

34

BY TRIP PAYNE

Answer on page 154.

ACROSS

1 ___ of Fire ('84 film)
8 Much ado
14 Fiduciary
15 Wins over, in a way
17 Exotic fruit
18 It won four Oscars
19 Terse affirmation
20 Piano virtuoso
22 Coll. degree
23 Lawrence ___, a.k.a. Mr. T
25 More advanced
26 Tolerable
27 Far East weight units
29 Erie hrs.
30 Name coined by George Eastman
31 Precipitous
33 Chengdu is its capital
35 Medieval quaff
37 Stocking stuffer?
38 Splash
41 "Stop already!"
45 *Tosca* role
46 Pull a fast one
48 Jazz keyboard player
49 Unimaginative
50 Honesty or dishonesty, e.g.
52 Story
53 Meadow butter
54 Fruit in a Prokofiev opera
56 Smidgen
57 Sold tickets, in a way
59 Cross one's heart
61 Scarlett or Antigone
62 Wake up, as a party
63 Winners in '69 & '86
64 Storks, at times

DOWN

1 Basseterre's island
2 Pearson's successor
3 Gossiped
4 ABA title
5 Decorative case
6 Worry
7 Sink to the bottom
8 Sealed
9 Studio sign
10 Asgard resident
11 Cob's companion
12 Dance of the '90s
13 Spirited steed
16 Carroll critter
21 Edge
24 51-card game
26 Way to leave a 76ers game
28 Take care of
30 Chaka and Aga
32 Producer Hiken
34 Cedar Rapids campus
36 Shames
38 Crusader's nemesis
39 Red, yellow, or blue
40 *The Longest Day* author
42 Serving to bring together
43 Jet or Shark
44 Becomes callous
45 Inspector Alleyn's creator
47 "Peanuts" character
50 Ecumenical Council site
51 Lead-and-tin alloy
54 Bee's grandnephew
55 Scale notes
58 *Mysterious Island* actor
60 Sch. founded in 1861

35

BY DEAN NILES

ACROSS

1 Most embarrassed
8 Philip II's fleet
14 Sabra
15 Pool item
17 Featured
18 Actress Parsons
19 Sennett lawman
20 Movie VIP
22 Layered rocks
23 Geraint's better half
25 "Did You Ever ___ Dream Walking"
27 Warplanes
28 Sups in style
30 ___ Lama
33 Prior to, to Prior
34 Author James and family
36 Happy Valley setting
38 Orthodontic devices
40 Broom closet items
43 Photo tint
46 Naval off.
47 Pique experiences
49 Kind
51 Total repulse
53 Starts to paint
55 Naldi of the silents
56 Least robust
59 Exec. branch board
60 Carol word
61 Fierce fighter
63 I specialist
66 Inveigles
67 Go off on a tangent
68 Navy builder
69 One with a wait problem

DOWN

1 Played with fire
2 Tartu's country
3 Couturier's concern
4 Org. founded in 1890
5 Chariot terminus
6 Runners carry them
7 Put in order
8 Sleeve contents
9 Bandleader Morgan
10 Certain Prot.
11 Nautical adverb
12 Lallygagged
13 Briskly, to Bizet
16 Not as significant
21 No-nonsense
24 Farm equipment name
26 King of comedy
29 Transudes
31 Burrows and Vigoda
32 Less than perf.
35 *Where Eagles Dare* weapon
37 Presidential cabin at Camp David
39 Jejune
40 Ezra, for one
41 Some fabrics
42 Mirror
44 It's sometimes embroidered
45 Public performer
48 Hazards a ticket
50 Pacific island
52 ___ incognita
54 *Full House* actor
57 Strike ignorer
58 Wrapping need
62 Literary monogram
64 Brutus's breakfast, maybe
65 Up to

36

by Shirley Soloway

ACROSS

1 Causing worry
10 She played Sofia
15 Song from *Aladdin*
16 Series of problems
17 City on the Nieuwe Maas
18 Pelvic bones
19 Hog-wild
20 Tried to discern
22 Baretta's bird
23 Beatles song
25 Spare part?
27 Sonnet conclusion
28 Thieves' headquarters?
29 Type option
30 Marat's spirit
31 A step in the right direction?
34 Wounds deeply
36 Continental opener
37 Brothers
38 Word on only one coin
39 Chinese plants
41 Runs
42 Speedy solution?
43 Form of silica
44 Word with dance or paint
45 Alphabetic sequence
46 *The Magnificent Seven* name
47 Parlor pastime?
51 Small matter?
53 Burmese building
55 Bartender on *The Simpsons*
56 Cronus or Oceanus
58 Marriage, e.g.
60 *Dallas* matriarch
61 Suggestions
62 Hardly ritzy
63 Schedules the nuptials

DOWN

1 Debug?
2 Metonymy or synecdoche
3 Formalities
4 Tolkien creation
5 Royal prop
6 Fine rain
7 Quarterback retreats
8 Mod ending
9 Some verse
10 WWII agcy.
11 Edith Giovanna Gassion
12 Enjoys oneself
13 Accord
14 Recliner features
21 Cuts carrots
24 Turn of phrase
26 Loading area?
29 Slat
31 Breaks up
32 You might give it a whirl
33 Alexander the Great's teacher
34 Mesa city
35 It has a cupule
37 Finish the job
40 Buck's partner
41 Rummy variety
44 Timid beachgoers
47 Sign of vacancy
48 "___ roll!"
49 The Jackson 5 + the 4 Seasons
50 Gaggle gals
52 Dust buster?
54 Dish out
57 Waterloo name
59 Director Browning

37

BY TRIP PAYNE

Answer on page 149.

ACROSS

1 Withdraws
8 Practice punching
12 Appealing to feeling
13 With one's beau
16 Revolutionary, sometimes
17 Alley target
18 Sp. title
19 Cape Cod produce
21 Winds
23 Act human
24 Gunn's girl
25 "___ o'clock scholar"
26 Colchis-bound vessel
28 PGA part
29 Litter's littlest
30 Pedestrians, old-style
32 Bus driver's request
36 Less agile
37 Employed perspective
39 Soapmaking supplies
41 "___ nome" (*Rigoletto* aria)
42 Speed away
43 Poet Wilcox
44 Used a pew
45 "___ say!" ("Listen!")
46 Antisocial behavior
50 Barracks feature
51 Beastly
52 Out of stock
54 Aggie's kin
55 Watchman
56 Ho-hum
57 Pen pals, half the time

DOWN

1 Telescope sighting
2 Retiree of a sort
3 Joint custodian
4 Bulge location, briefly
5 Compact items
6 Continuously
7 Dispensary stock
8 Dirty look
9 Late-night legend
10 Specifically for
11 Shooter's spot?
13 "Boy, I'm in trouble!"
14 Connection
15 Start of Massachusetts's motto
20 Cut a deal
22 Mime or mimic
26 P.M.'s
27 Underlying reason
28 Mus. adaptation
31 First name in architecture
33 Sore subject?
34 Opening number
35 Former *60 Minutes* name
38 Sitcom staff
39 Meteoric
40 In it together
43 Old English letters
44 Newspaper filler
45 "Mighty Quinn" writer
47 Vincent Lopez theme
48 Badgers
49 This, for one
53 Bottom fl.

38

BY RANDOLPH ROSS

Answer on page 151.

ACROSS

1 Some aircraft
10 Comice kin
14 *Fame* name
15 Danza's *Taxi* role
16 Develops
17 Worrier's risk
18 Genesis figure
19 Cloth merchants
21 Awful noise
22 Presidential prerogative
23 Three Dog Night hit
24 *Sports Illustrated*'s '92 Sportsman of the Year
26 Work without ___
27 Eye part
28 Back then, back when
30 Most sumptuous
32 With 50-Across, action movie of '85
35 Short streets
36 Slippery sorts
38 Lift upright
39 Cal. page start
40 Sighing phrase
42 It's good in a pinch
45 Graph starter
46 He speaks in German
48 Big ox
50 See 32-Across
52 *The Chronicles of Clovis* author
53 Schnauzer feature
54 Wide road
56 "___ Theme" ('65 tune)
57 Palatability
58 Linguist's abbr.
59 Treated as unimportant

DOWN

1 Sighted
2 Sagan's Muse
3 Oglala and Hunkpapa
4 Millstone
5 Vb. form
6 "Go ahead, see if ___!"
7 Snare sound
8 Linus Pauling's birthplace
9 Comparatively fresh
10 Blast
11 Quick look
12 Least lenient
13 Auto accessories
15 Eur. nation
20 Draw in
22 Pizazz
25 Shirley Temple role
27 *Star Trek* officer
29 Chihuahua wear
31 Strand
32 Capable of being proved
33 Too tidy
34 Stone worker
37 Confession, absolution, and penance
38 Hughes, for one
41 Cretan of old
43 Expected back
44 ___ break (rests)
46 Caesar et al.
47 Truthful James's creator
49 Second to none
51 27.34 grains
52 Having both oars in the water
55 Columnist Smith

39

BY TRIP PAYNE

ACROSS

1 *From Here to Eternity* author
11 Temper tantrum
14 Voters
16 Brown's league
17 In a group
18 Van Eyck or Vermeer
19 Realize
20 Stubborn sort
21 Hardly Einsteinian
23 Thresholds
25 "___ it goes"
26 It's sometimes turned
27 Contralto's colleague
29 Gordon Shumway's alias
32 Kermit's nephews?
34 Leading man?
36 Monty's milieu
37 Soaks up again
39 Div.
41 Still life subjects
43 He'll set you free
45 NBC comedy show
46 Bristles
48 Western sch.
49 Baldwin et al.
51 Carriage
52 Dorothy's gale
55 Alphabetic trio
58 Eastern cape
59 Eastern accessory
60 Rancor
63 Life of the party
64 Tastes
65 Cézanne's schnoz
66 Alienators

DOWN

1 Nelson's partner
2 Brings relief
3 Recycled, as coins
4 Word form for "outer"
5 Plato's hangout
6 Runs for one's life?
7 Trams transport them
8 Styron's Turner
9 Allen and Frome
10 Needs glasses, perhaps
11 Tasman discovery
12 Terrible name?
13 Actress Daly
15 Hindu honorifics
22 First zookeeper?
24 Calendar pg.
25 Types
27 Beatitudes start
28 JFK's U.N. ambassador
30 Longer odds
31 Independent contractor
33 Hockey Hall of Fame name
35 Vane dir.
38 *The Crying Game* star
40 Lack of certainty
42 Abandon
44 Neighbor of It.
47 *Lycée* and *collège*
50 It can be wicked
52 Hamlet's big brother
53 Tony's cousin
54 Fancy display
55 On any occasion
56 ___ song (cheaply)
57 Hollow
61 Eastern newt
62 MIT grad

40

BY RANDOLPH ROSS

ACROSS

1 King or queen
9 Equilibrium
15 Starting words
16 Lack
17 Throws off
18 Actress Donohoe
19 Fortune's start
20 Flower cluster
22 *All My Children*, e.g.: Abbr.
23 Roman alternative, for short
25 Give a hand?
26 Small change
27 "___ it!" ("Amen!")
28 Zinger
29 Narcs' successes
30 Tangles up
32 Songwriter Chaplin
34 Like Lovecraft
35 Three, proverbially
38 Santa illustrator
40 "___ Be Love?"
42 Small part
45 Hoople's expletive
47 Mrs. Addams's nickname
48 Served well against
49 Suitable
50 Fracas
51 Livy's lang.
52 Featherlike
54 Pitcher part
55 Isolated, maybe
57 Party mascot
59 Starting up
60 Statistician's concern
61 Shows disrespect to
62 Goldwyn discovery

DOWN

1 Victoria's Secret buy
2 Musical half-step
3 Like some ink
4 Actor Victor ___ Yung
5 Collectors' actions
6 Physical lead-in
7 They may be hidden
8 More probing
9 Plan to
10 Hardly exciting
11 Marilu, on *Evening Shade*
12 Uses intuition
13 Put right?
14 Maze entrances
21 Airport fleet
24 Ma Walton portrayer
26 Calf-length garment
28 Gatherings of sorts
29 Go up in smoke
31 "Later"
33 Part of USMA
36 Cedar eater
37 First down concern
39 It follows four, but not five
40 Language of Valencia
41 Abridge
42 Former Baghdad rulers: Var.
43 Locust tree
44 Quarter swallowers
46 *Palais des Nations* home
49 Some vases
50 Tintype color
52 Have longings
53 Arctic bird
56 Insult
58 Experiences

41

BY TRIP PAYNE

ACROSS

1 Dove, for one
5 Asset
9 Jumper's need
11 Awful bomb
13 Bar offering
14 Rifle
16 Subordinate Claus
17 Chaplin costar
19 Actress Clark
20 Word of woe
22 Kindergarten refrain
23 Daisy preceder
24 Crisp snack
26 Right-angle shape
27 Strikes, in a way
28 Franklin or Jefferson
30 Use a wok
32 Roman road
34 River to the North Sea
35 Table feature
38 Scrap, as a mission
41 Colorful perennial
42 Morse syllable
44 Front man
46 Hwys.
47 *Safety Last* star
49 Tropical tree
50 Ariz. neighbor
51 Heat sources
53 Nobel poet's monogram
54 Aristide, e.g.
56 Seven, on the Strip
58 Campaign highlight
59 Wonder Woman, by birth
60 Devil-may-care
61 Stewed state

DOWN

1 Sub command
2 ___ whim
3 Classical contest
4 Sri Lanka export
5 Basie's instrument
6 Set down
7 Fleet initials
8 Frolic about
9 Sinatra specialty
10 Creepy
11 Moral weakness
12 *Juno and the Paycock* playwright
13 English actor Edmund
15 Cartographer's dots
18 Alice's restaurant
21 Some Moslems
23 Bring down, as a priest
25 Appliance maker
27 Dobie Gillis's pal
29 Part of ITT
31 Stein connector
33 Hockey rink divider
35 European resort
36 Garret function
37 Brit's brig
39 Plant problem
40 Certain Sooner
41 Roguish
43 Pack member
45 Far East weight
47 Unwilling
48 Small shots
51 Slanting cut
52 Kenton of music
55 TV listing abbr.
57 Commando weapon

42

BY DEAN NILES

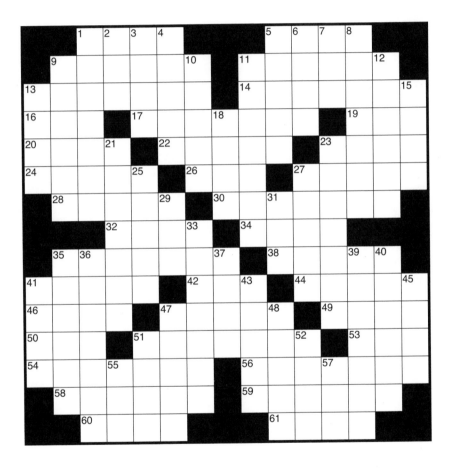

Answer on page 159.

ACROSS

1 Tan dreader
11 Vast amounts
15 Hunting time
16 Highly strung
17 Annual music festival
18 Folklore beast
19 Parisian pronoun
20 Passes on
21 Splash sound
23 "___ a song go ..."
25 Some rolls
26 Hawaii's state bird
27 Judges, at times
30 Chinese philosophy
31 Sundance's girlfriend
32 Actor Auberjonois
33 Ruhr city
35 Daytime offering
38 Less furnished
41 Felt awful about
42 Moolah
46 Oklahoma town
47 4 Seasons #1 tune
49 Kuwaiti royalty
50 Bipedal complement
52 Author Morrison
53 Chants
54 I ___ Fugitive From a Chain Gang
57 Bridget Fonda's uncle, once
58 Évian evening
59 Cook's call
62 Windshield option
63 Tied
64 Narrow advantage
65 Verbal abuse

DOWN

1 Emergency medium
2 Uniform feature
3 Soft
4 Verb ending
5 Nobel city
6 Cheat at pin the tail on the donkey
7 Turns left
8 Barcelona bear
9 Asset expert
10 Make beloved
11 Where to get off
12 Predators-to-be
13 Sky sights
14 Treats badly
22 Stage platform
24 Annoying sort
27 Singing syllable
28 Tyrannical
29 "Peace ___ time"
34 Former host of *America's Funniest Home Videos*
36 Mr. Bean
37 Last name in ice cream
38 Sheer fabric
39 Tonsil neighbor
40 In a rage
43 Having feeling
44 Grid group
45 Neptune's weapon
48 Followed, as advice
51 Rich cake
54 Siam visitor
55 Base repast
56 *Laugh-In* name
60 Grand Isl.'s locale
61 Pro ___

43

BY RANDOLPH ROSS

ACROSS

1 Lamarck or Linnaeus
10 Hägar's pet
15 Simultaneously
16 Barfly, perhaps
17 Quilts and comforters
18 Adventure movie set in the Andes
19 Have ___ for news
20 Emphasizes, one way
22 Author Deighton
23 Closely trimmed
26 Work in the mailroom
27 Toys with
29 Storm warnings
31 Hope on *thirtysomething*
32 Author Glasgow
34 Author Hanff
36 Words in a McCullers title
39 Chicken parts
40 Obtuse sort
41 TV host Jack and others
42 Jackson 5 #1 tune
43 Bestselling '73 autobio
45 Salinger title name
49 Actress Nettleton
51 Like wind chimes
53 252 gallons of wine
54 Guns
56 Big antelope
58 ___ hasty retreat
59 Carter budget director
62 Music category
63 *Falcon Crest* star
64 Nicholas Gage book
65 Cub leader

DOWN

1 Arnaz number
2 Actress Graff et al.
3 Satan
4 Varnish ingredients
5 Midwest Indians
6 State title: Abbr.
7 Chemical suffix
8 Put in writing, old-style
9 Professor, often
10 Part of Pisces
11 Lopez dedicatee et al.
12 Shining examples
13 Deeply respectful
14 Planking supports
21 Charm
24 Minim
25 On the safe side
28 Splinter group
30 Crystal gazer
33 Not of the clergy
35 Verb in optics
36 Like most mountains
37 Like opossum
38 Bring to ruin
39 Umpire's call
41 Gasoline derivative
44 Polyphemus's defeater
46 Stop the flow of
47 Ball State location
48 Fill with love
50 Glossy weave
52 Mello ___ (soft drink)
55 "The ___ Love"
57 *Café* additive
60 Didn't stay fast
61 Burns hero

44

BY TRIP PAYNE

ACROSS

1 ___ Brava (resort area)
6 Thin sheet
12 Gravy ingredients
14 Grid groups
16 Old Plymouth
17 It fell in 612 B.C.
18 "Put a lid ___!"
19 Indian River product
21 Latin lover's word
22 Bracken of cookbooks
23 Computer screen symbol
24 Pervasive quality
25 Swelled heads
27 Hardly secret
28 Sill sitter
29 World History period
31 Memorable ship
32 Botches up
33 *Show Boat* composer
34 Montana town
36 Yankees' #5
40 Comics kid
41 Our genus
42 Boot
43 Move slowly
44 Sapporo sport
45 Little guy
46 Pump abbr.
47 They come with strings attached
49 That: Latin
50 One who makes things possible
52 Running amok
54 Trattoria treat
55 Mean dudes
56 Daryl Hannah film
57 Western band

DOWN

1 L.A.'s La ___ Boulevard
2 Bond issuer, e.g.
3 Cut an opening in
4 Lapsang souchong, e.g.
5 ___ time (never)
6 Singing sister
7 Even up
8 Biblical wall word
9 "... de trouble ___ seen"
10 Ben Cartwright, for one
11 Buttercup family member
12 Felt one's way
13 Rank indicators
15 Pre-film feature
20 Old pros
24 Raccoonlike mammal
26 Rough outline
27 Cruel brute
28 Legal intro
30 Putting on aesthetic airs
31 Brief note
33 Geisha garb
34 Bonkers
35 Let go
36 Major-___
37 Cowardly
38 Set apart
39 Webbed-footed friends
40 Basil's movie partner
41 Supportive shout
44 Sir Patrick ___ (Scottish ballad subject)
47 Sole food
48 Kind of cookie
49 "How sweet ___!"
51 French formal dance
53 Ruckus

45

BY DEAN NILES

ACROSS

1 Scheria, today
6 Refractional
15 Guarantees
16 Membership
17 Transplant
18 Inexact numbers
19 Indonesian island group
20 Kevin of '80s and '90s baseball
22 Drive away
23 Inn type
24 Just things
26 Wee
27 At leisure
29 Uncovers
31 Roulette bet
32 *From Here to Eternity* extras
33 Inverness features
37 Pack
39 Seljuk, e.g.
40 Vaquero's gear
41 Angel's favorite letters
43 Thompson of *Family*
44 Ragtime dance
47 Beast of *Bürde*
48 Word before jump or lift
51 It may be underfoot
53 CD source
54 Onetime big name in tennis
56 Playa Azul locale
57 Hard-rock center
58 Detached
60 Squash tool
62 Keyboard technique
63 Clan symbol
64 Cosmetic ingredients
65 Bee's leftovers

DOWN

1 Mountaineer's ring
2 Finished
3 ___ de Venezuela
4 Back
5 Spanish I word
6 One way to get a lift
7 Video lines
8 Corporate trainee
9 Goes around
10 Melt-resistant product
11 Way over yonder
12 Puente and Jackson
13 Appendix neighbor
14 Pelota catcher
21 "___ Sing and I'm Happy"
25 Celebes Sea archipelago
28 Calliope's relative
30 Ad hoc band
34 Elegant ones
35 Hunting game
36 Colts, for instance
38 Asian capital
39 Finish the dirty work
41 Dried bouquet plant
42 Table requests
45 Ft. Presque Isle's site
46 *Lucia di Lammermoor* highlight
48 Ismail and Abbas I
49 Inoperative
50 Void
52 *Wayne's World* role
55 ___ *Troll* (Heine book)
59 ___ Block
61 Debt offering

46

BY JOE CLONICK

ACROSS

1 Platemaker's need
8 Tucson's ___ National Monument
15 Toledo native
16 Not as straight
17 Hardly
18 Touched
19 Lip-service product
20 Duct tail
22 Word in a '56 Broadway title
23 Trade
24 The butler in *Top Hat*
26 Frank outlet
27 Personality-change technique
28 Above water
30 Valentino title role of '26
31 Closet hang-up
33 Imposes, perhaps
35 It's black-and-white and read all over
37 Advance
40 Flat from fiction
44 "On New Democracy" author
45 Country hit of '68
47 Hammer holder
48 Formication by-product
50 Help heal
51 *Last of the Mohicans* locale
52 Set shots
54 Prune-processing chemical
55 Whence "pajamas"
56 ___ chicken
58 Roots
60 Debra's *Black Widow* costar
61 Where to catch some rays
62 Early filmmaker
63 Advocates

DOWN

1 Associates
2 Cut out
3 Mount
4 Camcorder capability
5 Points
6 Chi preceder
7 New Spain component
8 Jurisdiction
9 Norwegian trio
10 Play a round
11 In fast company?
12 Lacking a point
13 Change portions
14 Invests, in a way
21 Film score Oscar winner of 1970
24 Chemist/composer
25 Carry out
28 Tuscan, Messiah, or Dolphin
29 Rich treat
32 Novelist/semiotician
34 Forest role
36 Not as sound
37 Do
38 *War and Peace* heroine
39 Springtime site of song
41 Of interest to Adamson
42 *Gullible's Travels* author
43 ___ *and Models* ('55 film)
46 Famed forger
49 Song sung by Senators
51 Match
53 Grammatical form
55 Dolby flaw
57 *A Woman ___ Woman* (Belmondo film)
59 Maracana Stadium site

47

BY ERIC ALBERT

Answer on page 157.

ACROSS

1 London paper
9 Famous rider
15 Tom Selleck movie
16 *Daniel Boone* star
17 Continental rival
18 Show the way
19 Former chess master
20 *Roots* Emmy winner
22 Wearying sort
23 Put up with
25 Entanglement
27 Operatic princess
28 Merciless villain
29 Braille-writing need
32 Hall of Famer Williams
33 Major nation
35 *Bonanza* setting
37 Divine archer
38 Prelude follower
39 "The Dircaean Swan"
42 Suave person
46 G.P. gp.
47 Home of the brave?
50 ___ Gigio
51 Perlman and Howard
53 ___-Cone
54 Former Barbary State
55 Field worker
57 Jacob's daughter
60 Military inst.
61 Checks
63 Harlequin creations
65 Child's concern
66 Certain correspondence
67 Sowing machine
68 Oil

DOWN

1 Last words of "Harrigan"
2 Blood pigment
3 Pretty soon
4 Benzene base
5 24-book work
6 MCs' props
7 Israeli diplomat
8 Firm and tough
9 Embarrassed
10 Prepare for printing
11 Miscellany
12 Retired woman, perhaps
13 Went back
14 Poncherello's portrayer
21 Cath. or Luth.
24 Inspected, in a way
26 1950 Nobel winner
29 Nightly noises
30 QB's concern
31 ___ high standard
34 Smell ___
36 Taste for fine art
38 Sampras specialty
39 Holiday activities
40 Sid's partner
41 Actress Fabray
43 Certain angiosperm
44 Unisex
45 Antarctic arm
48 Close
49 Belgian sleuth
52 McCarthy's trunkmate
54 "Is ___ fact?"
56 Balsa or balsam
58 Fourth pig's amount
59 NYSE rival
62 *Guiding Light*, e.g.: Abbr.
64 Refusals

48

BY TRIP PAYNE

ACROSS

1 Tyrants
8 Oscar role for Streep
14 Globe line
15 Antecede
16 Under the table
17 Lasagna ingredient
18 Soft touch
19 Stooped (to)
20 From ___ Z
21 Lady of the lea
23 Brant and graylag
24 Baltic port
26 Stone and Gless
29 It can be eaten or drunk
31 1985 Kate Nelligan film
32 Police hdqrs.
35 Inner city business areas
38 Vane dir.
39 Eniwetok event
40 Idyllic abodes
41 Coin of Cairo
43 Nakskov native
44 Pale as a ghost
47 Apple cider girl
48 Understanding
49 Chest-related
52 Follower of Lao-tzu
55 Humorous
56 Popular cuisine
57 Colorful rings
58 Contract examiner
59 Awaited judgment
60 Agamemnon's son

DOWN

1 He thought, therefore he was
2 Mathematical propositions
3 Put in lieu of
4 Cut back
5 Midwestern tribe
6 Has a rough night
7 Mexican Mrs.
8 Barbra's *A Star Is Born* costar
9 Call on to speak
10 Loves unabashedly
11 Photo finish
12 Diminutive suffixes
13 Appropriately named novelist
15 Ante- kin
19 Down-to-earth
22 ___ *Poppa?*
25 Enzyme ending
27 Observed the Sabbath
28 Washington bill
30 Easily taught
32 Least candid
33 Waltz state
34 Yes-men
36 Child welfare org.
37 Unmatched
41 Lesson length
42 Pretty
44 Fall into ___ (get caught)
45 *The Godfather* star
46 Bonn breeches
50 Outfitted
51 Plural for -y, often
53 Frigid finish
54 Responsibility
56 USN rank

49

BY RANDOLPH ROSS

ACROSS

1 Frequent fliers
7 *A Thousand Clowns* Oscar winner
13 Measure of success?
14 Impression
16 '60s scent
17 He named Louisiana
18 Accumulated
19 Clydesdale cry
21 André's ex
22 Comic Gilliam
23 *City of Joy* star
25 Proper
26 Lucas character
28 *The Morning Watch* author
29 Mystery or history
30 Loose
32 Out of the woods
33 Animal secretion
35 What's happening
38 Key
41 Baloney type?
42 British piece
43 Sow chow
45 Stroller's spot
46 Put away
48 Start to cry?
49 Like-minded
50 Baby carrier?
51 Borders on
53 Texas town
55 Leto's daughter
57 Strip
58 Office extension
59 Strikes down
60 Bounded

DOWN

1 Super
2 Pass over
3 Shady character?
4 *Ensign Pulver* actor
5 UFO pilots
6 Rock lover
7 Its capital is Belmopan
8 *Poor Richard's Almanack* feature
9 Bodybuilder Rachel Mc___
10 Depot: Abbr.
11 Malady
12 Jean Baptiste Poquelin
13 Lit
15 Not as slovenly
20 Man of vision?
24 Pasty-faced
25 Postage devices
27 Elevated
29 Fellow
31 Swab salutation
32 "___ chance!"
34 Mongooses
35 Sang-froid
36 Runs the risk
37 Needle holder
39 Milk protein
40 Piratic activity
42 Gems
44 Band on the run
46 Rocker Winwood
47 Librarian's gadget
50 Blind part
52 Composer Bartók
54 Hibiscus garland
56 Criticize

50

BY DEAN NILES

Answer on page 151.

ACROSS

1 Claw up a cliff
9 High spirits
14 Past tense
15 King genre
17 Inquisition event
18 Fancy
19 Coronation *cité*
20 Former North Carolina senator
22 Crushed
23 Sedan seasons
24 Capp character
25 Cut back
26 Snake sound
27 Rise above it all
28 Nintendo name
29 Type var.
30 Lurch about
31 Friday drama
35 Buffalo
36 Brush alternative
37 Orchestra instrument
38 Plate place
39 Tolkien character
40 Lentil dish
43 Meerschaum part
44 High fidelity
45 *The Whales of August* star
46 ___ Aviv
47 Very selective eater
48 Music mark
49 Seasons
51 Man with a method?
53 Regular
54 And many, many more
55 Certain vertical
56 Last courses

DOWN

1 Parts with
2 Vinegar vials
3 Makes another bow
4 Rutherford's concern
5 Trundle and twin
6 Auto accessory
7 Bankhead movie
8 Sisyphean
9 Church group
10 Saddle part
11 Directional suffix
12 Crossword marks
13 Old phones
16 Hunting hound
21 Poodle pro
24 Let out, perhaps
25 Keeping
27 Punishes, as a leadfoot
28 Tropical fruit
30 Actress Williams
31 Like some measures
32 Contemptibly
33 Easter exclamation
34 Alluring, informally
35 Scholarly appendage
37 Bribed
39 Biblical fruit
40 Very selective eater
41 Own
42 Tibetan dogs, for short
44 Gnats and little brothers
45 Nettle
47 Caesarean section?
48 Corp. VIP
50 *Oedipus* ___
52 Dose units

51

BY DEAN NILES

ACROSS

1 Got wise, with "up"
10 Plus
15 Player's accomplishment
16 They may be square
17 Kitchen accessories
18 Sleep disorder
19 Through
20 Adams and McClurg
21 Snert's master
22 Cores, as of plants
24 Turow book
26 O'Grady of *Eight Is Enough*
27 Start of Massachusetts's motto
28 Inveigle
30 Actor Glass
31 Molinaro and Martino
33 "Blah, blah, blah"
35 *Treasure Island* extra
38 Run
39 Most gritty
41 Ruby or garnet
42 Groan producer
43 Fixes, as a stuffed animal
45 Followed suit
49 Unbalanced
51 Actress Allgood
52 Woodworking tool
53 Cut loose
55 Gossipy type
57 Maj.'s superiors
58 Puerto Rico, potentially
59 Among other things
61 Singer James et al.
62 Baseball program feature
63 Two-line dances
64 Carthage's locale

DOWN

1 Den of antiquity?
2 Take occupancy
3 Flags
4 Cartoon Chihuahua
5 What x may mean
6 Phillips University site
7 Ingenious device
8 ___ cordiale
9 Napoleon and others
10 Oriental nurse
11 Calyx part
12 Spanish drink
13 Powell and Parker
14 Winter Palace resident
23 Paid attention to
25 Punch spikers
28 Lauder et al.
29 Flaubert's father
32 Secret retreat
34 Basin type
35 One of Charlie's wives
36 Break new ground
37 Lamb, e.g.
39 Not as common
40 Roman playwright
44 Unrestrained
46 Third largest asteroid
47 Unabridged
48 Marquis ___
50 Corolla part
52 "Gay ___"
54 Minus
56 Gull relative
60 Cooling units, for short

52

by Trip Payne

ACROSS

1 Soprano Teresa
8 Quagga kin
13 Interoffice activity
15 Flip
17 Smack of
18 Agreeable sort
19 Nigerian town
20 Gourmet sensors
22 Work's worth
23 Short shots
25 U.S. Virgin Islands, e.g.
26 Salutation word
27 Log
29 Eur. airline
31 "... some kind of ___?"
32 Shapely
35 Sharp turn
37 Eliel's son
38 Mr. Scruggs
39 Moneybags
41 Went bad
44 Bolivian river
45 Health concern
47 "___ Family" ('79 hit)
49 Ford models
50 Antony's attendant
53 Meat concoction
54 NW state
55 Parable subject
58 Apron part
59 All there
61 Sole stuff
63 Underground retreat
64 Having ears
65 ___ voce
66 Guardian deities

DOWN

1 Fairyland denizen
2 Richie Cunningham's friend
3 Key stone?
4 Ninny: French
5 Certain worker
6 Sosa stat
7 *Maison* division
8 Mag industry suffix
9 Adam's grandson
10 Underwear brand
11 Timber evergreen
12 Rya, perhaps
14 Adapts
16 Midnight meeting
21 Carpentry and printing
24 Nobel poet
26 Quick quips
28 Tpks., e.g.
30 It'll put you in a lather
33 Provokes
34 Mahalia's music
36 Mushroom
39 Hard as a rock
40 Put up with
42 Seat device
43 New kid on the block
44 Light-headed one?
46 Conflict site
48 Lays in
51 Ahead
52 Put aside
55 Strained
56 Choral part
57 Quick trip
60 Word for Mitterrand
62 G.E. acquisition of 1986

53

by Dean Niles

Answer on page 157.

ACROSS

1 Alarmed by
9 Canterbury cleaners
14 Robert De Niro role
15 Legal property recipient
16 Did some math
17 Boeotia's neighbor
18 Metric measure
19 Dusty winds
21 *M*A*S*H* extras
22 Clears (of)
24 Actress Williams et al.
25 Naysayer
26 Freeze
28 *Emerald Point* ___
29 "Slammin' Sammy"
30 Rushlike plants
32 Be equivocal
34 Shrinking sea
36 MX structure
37 Word before Cup
41 Eastwood's town
45 King or Queen creation
46 Busy Apr. worker
48 Tool along
49 John Emerson's slave
50 Grinders
52 MacGraw and Baba
53 Kurosawa film
54 Carried aloft
56 Trio from San Antonio
57 More pernicious
59 Turtle shell
61 Napa Valley business
62 Female hormone
63 *Broca's Brain* author
64 Itchy

DOWN

1 Exotic trips
2 Jodie's '91 role
3 Gave in
4 Scoundrel
5 Homer's field
6 Column style
7 Kind of band
8 They're felt
9 "Memory" show
10 Buffet
11 Put in order
12 Narrative
13 Summer site
15 Outlaws
20 Hops dryers
23 Like pfeffernuesse
25 Its language is Catalan
27 Pauline's problem
29 Caesar, for example
31 Former USAF division
33 Ocasek of the Cars
35 Shoe tier
37 *Star!* star
38 Brno's region
39 Kind of dress or bag
40 Katharine's crony
42 Used car concern
43 Shows
44 Drops off
47 Colonel's command
50 Major, e.g.
51 Affects adversely
54 Swiss canton
55 Head line?
58 Perrins's partner
60 Campaigner, for short

54

by Trip Payne

ACROSS

1 Largest asteroid
6 They run hot and cold
13 "Thrilla" site
14 Chilean politician
16 Minute
17 Scheduling concern
18 ___ vult (Crusades cry)
19 Some terriers
21 ___ Tin Tin
22 Afr. country
23 Famous first baseman
24 ___ time (never)
25 Calcutta queen
27 Snag, as a cocktail frank
28 Propeller heads
29 They're wicked
30 Dirk Bogarde movie
32 Hunt and Hayes
33 Hale fellow
34 ___-car
35 Black Mountain poet
36 Checkerboard
40 Sitcom exec
41 Audits
42 Electronic memo
43 MIT grad
44 Netman Orantes
45 *Vogue* rival
46 Saracen weapon: Var.
48 Kind of soccer
50 Dugong or manatee
51 Sharecropper, e.g.
52 Casbah city
53 "Sailing to Byzantium" poet

DOWN

1 Connected series
2 "Stop, already!"
3 Outer limits
4 First name in gin?
5 Dieter's friend
6 Thin strips
7 President Franklin
8 Cockamamie
9 Mars and Mercury
10 U.N. Day month
11 Triskaidekaphobic obsession
12 Grad groups
13 *Call Me* ___
15 Drifts
20 Texas ___
23 Canea resident
24 Charm
26 Stick-in-the-mud?
27 Bambi's creator
29 Taffy trait
30 Navel alternative
31 Introductory remark
32 *Siddhartha* author
33 ___ than (at least)
34 Vote count
36 Aural impediment
37 At sea
38 Crow's toes
39 Put out
41 *Parade* composer
44 Quant creation
45 Irish novelist O'Brien
47 Actress Ryan
49 Eleanor Roosevelt ___
   Roosevelt

55

BY DEAN NILES

ACROSS

1 Cellar selections
6 Starves
14 Early computer
15 Field event
16 Actress Berger
17 Yankee, for one
18 Letters of credit?
19 Community leaders
21 Southeast Asian
22 Sgt., for one
23 Lead on
24 Shaving site
25 Shocked reaction
27 Cattle
28 Tea type
29 Cooking technique
31 He gets down to work
32 Vietnamese money
33 Actress Anderson
34 Made out
36 Gobi's country
40 Customs
41 Jakarta's island
42 Rat pack
43 Overestimates, e.g.
44 Onetime Atari rival
46 Actress Clarke
47 Prince in *Aladdin*
48 WKRP station manager
49 Unpropitious
50 Bill Withers recording
52 Ava ex
54 *Flashdance* theme singer
55 Mortgages, for example
56 Extended
57 Rich supplies

DOWN

1 Does an encore, perhaps
2 Baseball variation
3 Winding
4 Wolf down
5 Scenic view
6 Dam activity
7 Region on the Rhine
8 Leeds length
9 *Concord* composer
10 Italian isl.
11 Barbarous
12 Bess's predecessor
13 Call to a crew
15 Hard hitting
20 Similarly
24 Alumnus-to-be
26 California team
28 BB-gun sound
30 Bar on *The Simpsons*
31 Rainier place
33 "Who ___, baby?"
34 Desolate
35 Made it
36 Wild duck
37 Incorporated, in Ipswich
38 Queued up
39 Forever young
40 Cape Town corn
41 Hashemite kingdom
44 Dixon's colleague
45 ___ fours
48 Singer Laine
51 Adjective suffix
53 Copacabana city

56

BY TRIP PAYNE

ACROSS

1 Very, very old
9 Ruth stats.
12 Like most volcanoes
13 Lovebird
15 Rocker Eddie
16 Lymph gland location
18 Future falcon
19 Guy Williams series
21 Plow pioneer
23 Celtic
24 "Stuff and nonsense!"
25 Brit. mil. honor
26 Raison d'___
28 Wooden strip
29 *Tosca* tenor
31 Nebraska river
33 Annual honoree
37 Car wash workers
38 Logician Kurt
39 Of a time period
40 Graphic stuff?
41 Hockey legend
44 Tach reading
45 Adoption org.
47 Nerd
49 Election night data
53 Actress Sara
54 You
55 Da Vinci and Michelangelo
57 Exigencies
58 Trattoria orders
59 KLM rival
60 Indefinite answer

DOWN

1 Jitterbugged
2 Of recent vintage
3 Places for pots
4 Wagnerian exclamation
5 Musty
6 Husk hamper?
7 Currier's crony
8 Pivot point
9 Buttermilk, e.g.
10 Act like a kid
11 Come between
13 Soup holders
14 Lasagna ingredient
17 Rover's restriction
20 Bring to a boil?
22 "The Desert Fox"
26 Marine fliers
27 *Padre's hermano*
28 Knock down
30 It's held by Swiss banks
31 Third degrees?
32 Appomattox signatory
33 Nerds
34 Ahab's weapon
35 Models
36 Rug rat
40 Unlike this ans.
42 Send back
43 Check, as a chestnut
45 Husky hauls
46 Nicklaus numbers
47 Character in *Medea*
48 Lowdown singer?
50 Eye part
51 Oklahoma native
52 *Bounty* crew
56 Faraday's concern

57

BY RANDOLPH ROSS

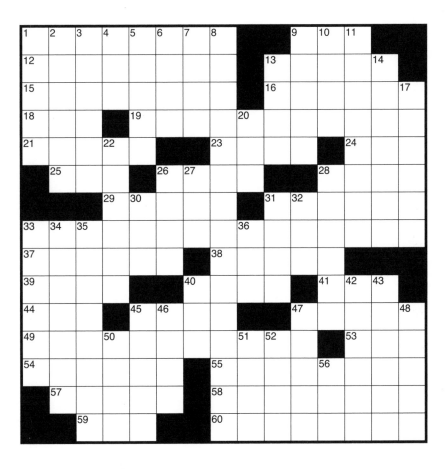

ACROSS

1 Beatles tune
8 Takes off
15 Some tanks
16 Rubout?
17 Really dull
18 Mosque feature
19 *Cheers* character
20 Peanut butter platform
22 H.S. exam
23 Birdsong of basketball
25 Nervous chuckle
26 Meanie's motive
28 Lerner's partner
30 Part of MIT
33 Always
34 Senator Hatch
35 Reached over
37 *How Green Was My Valley* author
40 Quinine target
42 Slither slyly
46 "Smooth Operator" singer
47 In addition
49 Sign up
50 Athletic exchange
52 ___ *pro nobis*
54 Movie maven Siskel
55 Mensa stats
56 Praise to the rooftops
60 Turkish chieftain
61 Visceral decision
63 Footstool
65 Had coming
66 "___ Lover!" ('55 hit)
67 Colorful bushes
68 Guayaquil's locale

DOWN

1 *Star Wars* character
2 It's in the doldrums
3 More munchable
4 Bowe blow
5 *Battle Cry* author
6 Kitchen denizen of song
7 Aerie infant
8 Moore of movies
9 "___ *go bragh*"
10 Bohr and Brahe
11 Dos Passos opus
12 Script
13 Picked up the tab
14 Sporting dog
21 "'Tis ___ ..."
24 Gulped down
27 Scribe's activity
29 In the: French
31 Sgt.'s subordinate
32 March or Roach
36 Wall St. initials
38 Tide rival
39 Wheaton of *Stand by Me*
40 Nobelist Gabriel García ___
41 Start of Kansas's motto
43 Fantasized
44 In days of yore
45 *My Day* name
46 It's a shame
48 Baltimore batter
51 Put on cloud nine
53 Montezuma, for one
57 Anatomical sections
58 Onetime Ford competitor
59 Words of accusation
62 Word form for "eyelash"
64 Medical suffix

58

BY MATT GAFFNEY

ACROSS

1 Onetime Woolery show
9 Puzzle variety
14 Spanish export
15 Second ___ (superior)
16 Settled the score
17 Get a horseshoes do-over
18 Double-play man
19 Finals prelims
21 *Give ___ Sailor* ('38 film)
22 Waldorf-Astoria muralist
23 ___ in the bucket
24 Ski maneuver
25 Refrain sound
26 Deacon's wear
27 Carol start
28 Like a peacock
29 Terrier threats
30 First name in waltzes
32 Strapping
33 Rake over the coals
34 Ruffle
35 Actress Worth
36 Goes quickly
37 Pasty-faced
40 Monotone, maybe
41 Dressed like an egghead
42 Celebrity kicker
43 Hit tune of 1970
44 Mythical weeper
45 "___ Street Blues"
46 Arcing football pass
48 Beside oneself
50 Patterned linen
51 Eveready competitor
52 Make pig iron
53 *Jungle Fever* director

DOWN

1 Most painful
2 Sharp as a tack
3 Spanish muralist
4 Head off
5 Kingsley and Cross
6 Peat's place
7 Proposes to repose
8 Advanced
9 Some deer
10 Otorhinolaryngology, for short
11 Explosive growth area?
12 Not in good taste
13 Opening words?
15 Junket
20 Comic Howard
23 In accord
24 Grouch's grimace
26 Portland cement element
27 Language exams
28 Do extremely well
29 Well-sooted?
30 Napa vessel
31 Knocked out
32 Upset
33 Lewd dudes
34 Outlaws
36 Frat house, at times
37 Animal in a pop song?
38 Certain gene
39 Crewel tool
41 Actor Benedict
42 Pound change
44 Settle in
45 Nuthatch's nose
47 Good buddy
49 Dernier ___ (latest style)

59

BY TRIP PAYNE

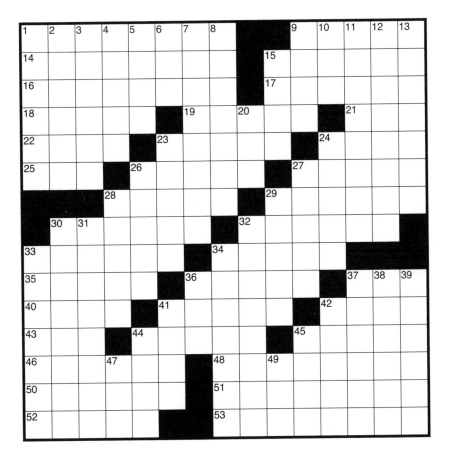

ACROSS

1 Mustang developer
11 A question of identity
14 Screwdriver part
16 Lady lobster
17 Jersey nickname
18 Make budget cuts?
19 Ratio words
20 Midwestern sight
21 IA hours
23 Co. head
24 Mountain lions
25 Tina's *30 Rock* role
27 Pounces on errors
28 Got hip, with "up"
30 Gilmore of basketball
31 Wyoming tribe
33 Hot spot
35 Sounding like Daffy
36 Unfamiliar
37 Longed (for)
38 REM vocalist
39 On ___-to-know basis
40 Harry's successor
41 Hungarian national hero
42 Palindromic town
45 MGM motto word
47 He's fabulous
48 Wingspread
49 Actress Benaderet
51 House of Lords, e.g.
54 Smith of Rhodesia
55 One of the Great Ones?
56 Help a waiter
57 Emerson, but not Thoreau

DOWN

1 Clear thinking
2 Use the delete key
3 Keep an ___ the ground
4 European beginning
5 Season
6 Criticizing
7 *The Naked Gun* actor
8 Sailor sword
9 Bologna byes
10 Pretense
11 "You heard ___!"
12 Pennsylvania Dutch barn symbol
13 In accord
15 Common Mkt.
22 Made a misstep
24 Henri's homeland
26 *Sieben + drei*
27 Ivy, for instance
28 Laundered
29 Checkers, e.g.
30 Dutch dialect
31 *Cry, the Beloved Country* author
32 Frequent game show "parting gift"
33 Questionables
34 Phrase of denial
39 Up
41 To the same degree
42 In pieces
43 Old Romania
44 "___ all of the above"
46 Mineo or Maglie
48 Sp. ladies
49 Formula catcher
50 It's in the Seine
52 Rizzo the ___ (Muppet)
53 Dollar divs.

60

BY Matt Gaffney

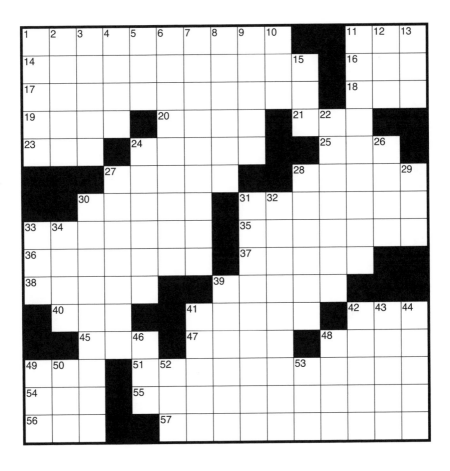

ACROSS

1 Roaring '20s
8 Something fishy?
14 Cranked out notions
15 Catalyst
17 Mixes at a mixer
18 Ceramics
19 Center starter
20 Family car
22 "Far out!"
23 "___ worry!" (calming words)
26 Folk tail?
27 Slalom obstacle
28 Score note
30 Weed killer
32 More piquant
34 Sullies
35 Word form for "soil"
36 Being abroad
37 Unoriginal thinkers
39 Treat with contempt
43 Tyrannize
45 More expensive
46 Butts
47 Southwestern st.
49 List of candidates
50 *Wheel of Fortune* purchase
51 Prerecorded
53 Beak, in Bordeaux
54 Florida town
57 Put on a new coat
60 Basis for comparison
61 Ennoble
62 Picnic areas
63 More tranquil

DOWN

1 Dana character
2 Fatty
3 They're tops
4 Change direction
5 Part of A&P
6 Adolescent exclamations
7 Ike-era auto
8 Put yolks in one bowl
9 Cleared
10 Hop to it
11 Island in the stream
12 Repetitive
13 Changes an assessment
16 Rig renter
21 Follow closely
24 Straw mats
25 Starting site
27 All-around
29 Fraction's alias?
31 Sad songs
33 ___ *Baby*
37 In pain
38 Base
40 Spirited steed
41 Kissinger accomplishment
42 Man of steel?
43 Theater offering
44 Agt.
48 Sherry city
52 Take out of print
55 Carte preceder
56 '60s chic
58 According to
59 "Hello, Cicero!"

61

BY RANDOLPH ROSS

ACROSS

1 Hymenoptera member
5 Keyboard feature
13 Luke's sidekick
15 Leisure periods
16 One who corners
17 Turns off
18 Pine product
19 China locale
21 One side
22 *"Ich bin ___ Berliner"*
23 Gave zip to
24 It may be posted
25 Mellowed
27 Washington collection
28 Gravity, e.g.
29 Lying fallow
31 Gauchos' gear
32 Foie ___
33 Spike supports?
34 Non-secular
37 Night spot?
41 Body of evidence
42 Bonny child
43 Properly balanced
44 Collectible descriptor
45 Bond portrayer
47 JVC competitor
48 Sullivan and McMahon
49 Miner's tool
50 Imogene's partner
51 View on news
53 Grate stuff
55 Like Frost's roads
56 River to the Mediterranean
57 Court shoes
58 Singer James

DOWN

1 *Embarkation for Cythera* painter
2 Bring to court
3 Novelist Laurence and family
4 Raven maven?
5 Wired fixtures
6 Patriot Thomas et al.
7 Thin as ___
8 Word on only one U.S. coin
9 Character in the *Iliad*
10 Walk-on
11 *West Side Story* song
12 Does some cobbling
14 Mythical monsters
15 Ancient Italians
20 Footless
24 Betters oneself?
26 Extent
28 Dumas, to Dumas
30 Big times
31 Ted Williams's team
33 Psychology school
34 Long diatribes
35 Disney blockbuster
36 Handwritten
37 Albania, Bulgaria, et al.
38 Hearing distance
39 Like the Sphinx
40 Lowest lake
42 More frilly
45 Poem of lament
46 Approach
49 Barbecue favorite
52 Manchester meal
54 Pronoun for Sean Young

62

BY TRIP PAYNE

ACROSS

1 Improvise
8 Bounds
15 Erstwhile
16 High point
17 Quarterback, often
18 Light source
19 Govt. research agcy.
20 Conformist
22 Panama pair
23 Crooning couples
25 Corrupt
26 Quote
27 Propelled a shell
29 *Wayne's World* word
30 Scarlett's suitor
31 Geriatric
33 Hipsters' opposites
35 Compensation
36 Battleship letters
37 Leader of the House
41 Cools it
45 Soupçon
46 Dulles abbr.
48 California Franciscan
49 Major conclusion?
50 Action times
52 Rights
53 Pressure meas.
54 Core material
56 Eastern sch.
57 His feast day is February 9
59 Do a voice-over
61 Spanish blades
62 Con man
63 Labor-intensive
64 Match makers?

DOWN

1 Unknown one
2 Out of the ordinary
3 *Indecent Proposal* star
4 Acct.'s abbr.
5 Lunar valley
6 "Experiment to me is everyone ___": Dickinson
7 Place that's also an anagram of "Meg Ryan"
8 Fixes a fracture
9 Housewarming gift
10 Went off
11 Multinational corp.
12 More strapped
13 Throttle: Var.
14 Western sights
21 "O Sole ___"
24 Cellar problem
26 Danced, in a way
28 *Golden Hind* captain
30 Decays
32 Percolation product
34 Who, to Richelieu
37 ___ it (hurries)
38 Break in a race
39 Name, as a work
40 Popular bloom
41 Proverbial wisdom
42 Mandrill, e.g.
43 Judge
44 Tea pros
47 Do road work
50 Cyclades isle
51 Impolite look
54 Mutt moniker
55 War of 1812 site
58 Always, to Arnold
60 Former NFL stadium

63

BY DEAN NILES

ACROSS

1 High-pressure place
9 License
15 John Doe
16 John and Priscilla
17 Tomato sauce
18 Actress Donohoe
19 Winged
20 Good buddies
22 Not vert.
23 Easy stride
24 Some sodas
25 Timbuktu's land
26 Chemical ending
27 More appealing
28 Fills the hold
29 *Ghostbusters* actor
30 "I ___ a clue!"
31 Diabolical
34 University officers
35 Support group
36 Fiend
37 Prima ___
38 Bull penners
39 Grass roots place
42 Keynes's subj.
43 Director Joshua
44 Elisabeth of *Back to the Future Part II*
45 Arrest
46 Harebrained trick
47 Not quite right
48 Ross Island volcano
50 Mythical racer
52 N.T. author
53 Held out
54 Marketeer
55 Strand

DOWN

1 Hen or pen
2 Barry Levinson movie
3 Colorful wrap
4 Less than fresh
5 *Fatal Attraction* director
6 Cold war gp.?
7 Stupefacient
8 Makes possible
9 '50s TV host and family
10 End of an O'Neill title
11 Vitamin bottle abbr.
12 Shad lookalike
13 Very lazy
14 Nicholas's supporters
21 Canal zone?
24 Parsley relative
25 Specialist
27 Algonquin transport
28 Nigeria's former capital
29 Arrested
30 Bruisers
31 Freedom from harm
32 Menu phrase
33 Fast-food franchise
34 Clever banter
36 Marks, as a page
38 Noise at an opening
39 Japanese religion
40 Expulsion
41 Marquis of note
43 Light heavyweight?
44 Tennis tactic
46 Salad veggie
47 Noted boxing family
49 Part of APB
51 Simile center

64

BY TRIP PAYNE

ACROSS

1 Brisk exchange
10 Lost
15 Rose magically
16 Scott's namesakes
17 Some natives
19 Former Mideast initials
20 Store name
21 Lower digit
22 Word in brackets
23 Tina of *30 Rock*
24 They deliver the goods
27 Organic compound
29 Wilderness forts
30 Bk. of the Bible
32 Hockey great
33 "... who lived in ___"
34 Sec
36 Cribbage piece
37 Nuremberg negatives
38 Pool
39 Ooh's mate
40 French department
41 Fast-food pioneer
43 Cratchit and Considine
46 State beforehand
47 CSA fighter
50 ___ de plume
51 D.C. figure
52 "Let ___ Be Your Umbrella"
54 Ex-communications co.
55 Authority figure
59 K.T. of country
60 Designs, as a bridge
61 Point ___, California
62 Treat, as dungarees

DOWN

1 Contract section
2 Stay behind
3 How the cocky act
4 Lady's man?
5 Packing a wallop
6 Prima ___ evidence
7 NATO member
8 Actor Auberjonois
9 Philip's dukedom
10 Contribute
11 Sect starter
12 "America, the Beautiful" phrase
13 Underground TV role?
14 Rates
18 Straight
25 Old toothpaste brand
26 Go berserk
28 ___-center (liberal)
29 Mountain nymph
31 Hysterical predator?
32 Changes colors
34 ___ joy (shows elation)
35 Raise
42 Rent-___
44 Takes a spin
45 James Bond opponent
47 A Starr
48 Like a sprite
49 Geoffrey of fashion
53 Big Sky st.
56 Move fast
57 Pulver's rank: Abbr.
58 Suture

65

BY RANDOLPH ROSS

ACROSS

1 Split apart
9 Farm animal
15 Playground competition
16 From C to C
17 Language final
18 *Macbeth* trio
19 Sea changes
20 Terse verse
22 "Can't Help Lovin' ___ Man"
23 Homeric genre
24 Gym name
25 Betz who won an Emmy for *Judd for the Defense*
26 M.A. or M.D.
27 Painter/inventor
28 Weather balloon
29 Make money
30 Spirited sessions?
32 Alert again
35 Fusses with feathers
36 Dean's list determinant
38 Beseeches
39 Come around
40 Midafternoon
42 Wrinkled dog
45 Actress Raines
46 *Henry & June* name
47 Adjust an Amati
48 Gist
49 Outfield surface
50 Hobbit name
51 Sharp scolding
53 Snuck up on
55 *A Sentimental Journey* writer
56 Caustic
57 Body types
58 Helpful chemicals

DOWN

1 Kicked (out)
2 Green
3 Quint or Popeye
4 Lacquered metalwares
5 Tolkien creatures
6 Deer lady
7 Strong, à la Samson
8 Corolla parts
9 Pawns
10 Stocking shade
11 Skater Midori
12 Burlesque performance
13 *Our Miss Brooks* star
14 Impatient
21 Bad day for Caesar
24 Auction word
25 Traffic pylons
27 Diver's hazard
28 Noncom
29 Former HUD secretary Hills
31 Fencing choices
32 Singularity
33 Assess
34 Mannerly, maybe
37 Italian erupter
38 Become angry
41 Armored catfish
42 One way to park
43 Straightened
44 Hollow rocks
46 Rhone city
47 Dame, e.g.
49 Peter the private eye
50 Flatter oneself
52 Brother's title
54 FBI abbr.

BY TRIP PAYNE

ACROSS

1 Sporty cars reintroduced in 2009
8 Advance
15 Early TV name
16 Iliescu's country
17 Actress Holm
18 Slippery sorts
19 It may be abstract
20 Clear, as a fence
22 Chou En-___
23 South Vietnamese leader
25 Baseball's Alejandro and Tony
26 Bluish green
27 Hard on the nose
29 "Agnus ___"
30 Odense residents
31 Got smart
33 Most lustrous
35 Get top billing
37 Nintendo rival
38 Built with beams
42 Hat part
46 *Oklahoma!* aunt
47 Talk on and on
49 Flight segment
50 Leave off
51 Rivera work
53 Rights gp.
54 Comparative ending
55 Strikes out
57 Poet Hughes
58 Blood count?
60 Steak style
62 Siren
63 Quarterback Boomer
64 Clinton spokesperson Myers et al.
65 Way down

DOWN

1 Summer hummers
2 Admiral Byrd's monoplane
3 Crabs and snakes
4 Sharpen, as cheddar
5 Hebrew letter
6 Numero uno's place
7 Trickled
8 Overcomes adversity
9 Emulates Sinbad
10 Ike's ally
11 Beyond balmy
12 Like a narrow bridge
13 Philippics
14 Most basic
21 They're exchanged for change
24 Faux pas
26 Asian capital
28 Check
30 Ballerina painter
32 ___ es Salaam
34 Shoebox notation
36 Usual crowd
38 Dwelt
39 Plant community
40 Blooming
41 "Make my day!," e.g.
43 Glucose-producing enzyme
44 Wing thing
45 Sensible
48 Took some cuts
51 Rumble
52 Rental agreement
55 Mussolini moniker
56 Indian titles
59 *El* ___ (Heston flick)
61 Tic-___-toe

67

BY FRED PISCOP

Answer on page 149.

ACROSS

1 Lash lengthener
8 Comes out ahead of
13 Vaccine containers
14 Marks on parcels
17 Fast fish
18 Examining
19 Vane reading
20 Like Fred Astaire
22 Opera prop
23 "A miss ___ good ..."
25 Sib's kid
27 Concerning
28 *Rabbit* ___ (Updike novel)
30 Manchester measure
32 Pool need
33 Collect on a surface
35 Young hares
37 Mouths to feed
39 Dreadful
40 Hibachi dish
44 Likely
48 Viking weapon
49 Nasty
51 Bungled
52 Adoption agcy.
54 "A friend in need is ___"
56 Line of clothing
57 Doughnut shape
59 Director Almodóvar
61 Word in a Heyerdahl title
62 Highbrow
64 Baking dish
66 Coffee utensil
67 Indigenous language
68 Movie scenes
69 Bounds

DOWN

1 Rich wine
2 Laid up
3 Peanut butter and jelly
4 Reduce, as a roster
5 Pub quaffs
6 Summer fare
7 Revile
8 Split
9 SASE, e.g.
10 Big deals
11 Melanie's mom
12 Discipline
15 Bogged down
16 Comes around
21 Salome's accessory
24 Finland, to Finns
26 Forage plant
29 They go right through you
31 Chilling
34 Serengeti sahib
36 Parents
38 Vere and Bligh
40 Preferences
41 Market abroad
42 Muster in
43 ___ *fixe*
45 Interrupt
46 Acting like a sieve
47 Spenser and Muskie
50 Apocrypha book
53 Actress Lindley
55 Chaplin role
58 *Written on the Wind* director
60 Hebrew measure
63 Links area
65 "___ tu" (Verdi aria)

68

BY DEAN NILES

Answer on page 151.

ACROSS

1 Crimson Tide
5 Certain crustaceans
14 *Dynasty* star
16 Sporty import
17 Sad piece
18 It's spotted at Westminster
19 Fond du ___, Wisconsin
20 Rent, e.g.
22 Actress Wedgeworth
23 ___ Z
24 Starch sources
25 Rose's love
26 Listing of courses
28 Caesar and Vicious
29 Beef tenderloin
30 "The Voice"
32 Arm-twisting
33 Man with a manor about him
34 Radiation quantities
35 One of the Gorgons
38 "___ My Heart for You" ('30 tune)
41 Break off
42 Obscenity
43 Dice
45 "Nuts!"
46 Fished en masse
48 Record label
49 Bastille Day season
50 Football liner
51 Bog
52 Full-spectrum
54 Dostoevsky figure
56 Flock of cardinals?
57 Obscenity
58 All, for one
59 "My Cup Runneth Over" singer

DOWN

1 Wild scene
2 Flies
3 1909 Nobelist in Physics
4 Geom. term
5 Jackie's successor
6 San Francisco neighbor
7 Broncos, e.g.
8 Consigns to perdition
9 Political suffix
10 "Baloney!"
11 Sweet-tempered
12 Brownie toppers
13 Lines from Shakespeare
15 Autumn abbr.
21 ___-Prussian War
25 Bag of wind?
27 Conditional conjunction
29 Be in a lather
31 Tiptop
32 Creditor
34 Most Pickwickian
35 Fastened
36 4:00 P.M.
37 Quick review?
38 Teensy bit
39 Cruise film
40 Unspecified person
42 Rap session?
44 They're spotted in Westerns
46 Street talk
47 Wet blanket
50 Harris title
53 Compass pt.
55 Edmond O'Brien thriller

69

BY TRIP PAYNE

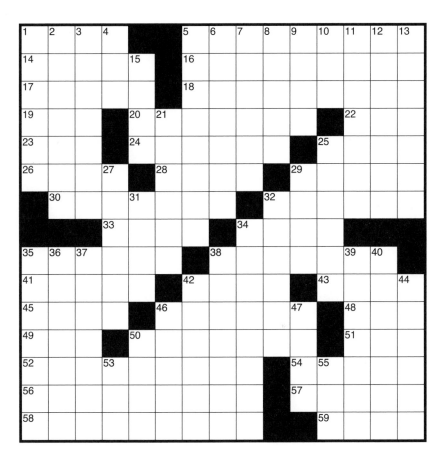

ACROSS

1 Editor of *The Wall Street Journal* crossword
10 Poet laureate decliner of 1813
15 Debussy classmate
16 *The Name Above the Title* autobiographer
17 Cipher
18 Top
19 Member of a frequently forbidden trio
20 Syrup source
21 Bring back
22 Letter of credit?
23 Start of a Rohmer film title
25 LBO aide
26 Slip
28 Cashier
29 Jackson of jazz
30 King victim
32 Way
34 Ancient craft
37 Not as sharp
38 Oscar role of '83
39 Kyongsong's other name
40 Teammate of Red and Enos
41 Days' beginning
43 Led Zeppelin title word
47 Ophidian outburst
48 Pessimistically
50 ORD datum
51 Natural earth
53 It may be called
54 Crosses of a sort
55 Hardly bashful
56 Ruth or Aaron, but not Mantle
58 Strike out
59 Goose
60 Tears
61 #1 song of '63

DOWN

1 Sword of Damocles
2 Mangle
3 Hans *und* Fritz, e.g.
4 Lengthens, old-style
5 One form of ID
6 Deck device
7 Origin
8 Air pollution adjective
9 *Treatise on Money* author
10 Cast off
11 Staff
12 Flexibility of a sort
13 Fast
14 Utility concern
23 Anchorman's ancestor
24 First name in neorealism
27 Obie winner of '70
29 ___ Park
31 Concession
33 Spring
34 Ignore
35 Beat
36 Disposal unit
37 Bill of Rights phrase
39 Jane's sister in *Stanley and Iris*
42 Like Archimedes
44 Where the fuchsia bloom
45 Circumnavigating sub of '60
46 Whodunit name
48 City founded by Julius Caesar
49 Goes berserk
52 "Once she did hold the gorgeous ___ ..."
54 Staff symbol
57 Lynne, Bevans, and Tandy

70

BY ERIC ALBERT

Answer on page 155.

ACROSS

1 Some sadists
9 *Black Money* hero
15 Abyssinia, today
16 File
17 Support of a sort
18 Volcano discovered in 1841
19 Goes through
20 Platonic Academy founder
21 Port ___, Washington
22 Epithalamic
23 Lady Lou's love
24 Net holding
25 *Playtime* name
26 Hail
29 Persian, for one
31 Winnie and Herbert's boy
32 Slow in scoring
34 Sin preceder
35 Polymerization product
36 Elliott of *Groundhog Day*
37 First name in cartooning
39 Center of attention?
40 Try
41 Barker of film
42 Coup victim of '62
44 Brutus Jones, e.g.
46 Started up the old way
50 Trade
51 Not alone
52 Took effect
53 Expecting
54 Move on a screen
55 Ace
56 Slight
57 Some Olympians

DOWN

1 Brilliant swimmer
2 "___ a hundred years ...":
Holmes
3 Emmy winner of '87
4 Brushed a ball
5 Bradbury Science Museum
city
6 Kind of pronoun
7 Curling teams
8 Hangs loose
9 *Australopithecus* member
10 Thinner
11 Firm, at times
12 Class M, to Kirk
13 Masters specialty
14 Hardy
22 Koussevitzky's successor
24 Fireproofing material
26 Lead changer
27 Fire
28 Send
30 Pilsen product
31 Mickey Rooney's girlfriend in
a '42 film
33 Jack's partner
38 Entry chamber
41 Grand
43 Lie back
45 Line holders
46 Where locks are installed
47 Burton role of '77
48 Reaction result
49 Conveyance requirements
51 Creature comforts

71

BY ERIC ALBERT

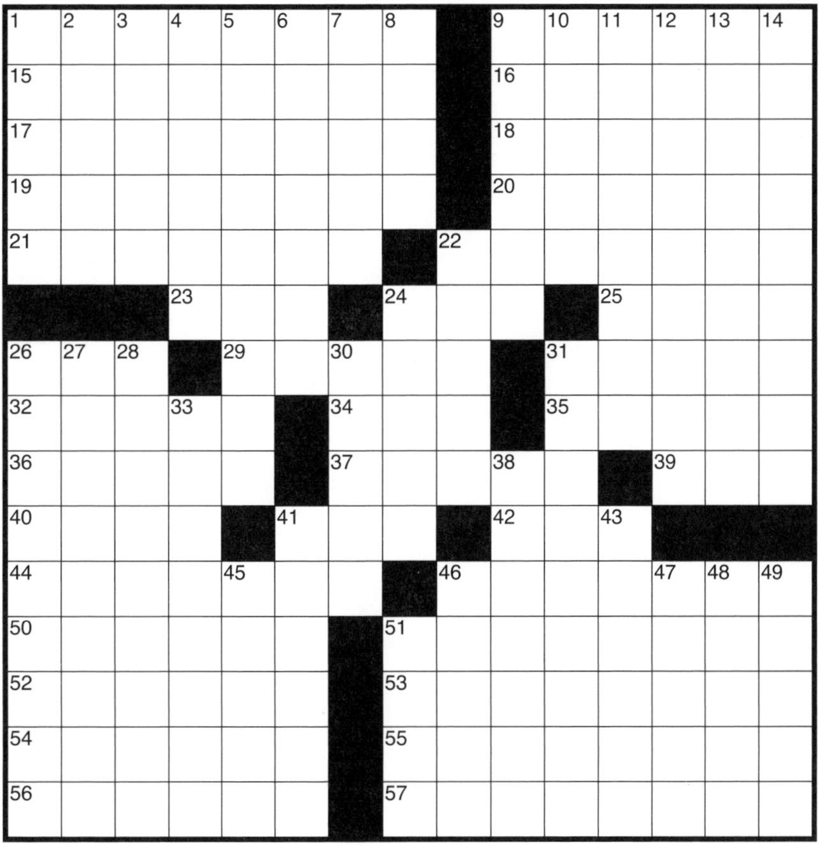

Answer on page 157.

ACROSS

1 *Boner's Ark* wife
8 Trade route of a sort
15 Conventionally
16 More on the stick
17 ARM provision
18 *The Self and Others* author
19 Vanity case
20 Harmonize with
21 Like some leaves
22 Unbridled
23 European Union member
25 Kovacs's first TV job
29 Scott, for one
34 *M*A*S*H* set
36 McQueen persona
37 *East of Eden* name
38 Lawyer/novelist
39 Acts name
41 Bear, in a way
42 *Up to* ___ ('50s game show)
43 Hugo's genre
45 Carpenter response
46 Fit
52 Jar
56 U.S. 101 terminus
57 ___ zone
58 Hot
59 Echo
60 *An American in Paris* soloist
61 Like rhodonite
62 Revolution period

DOWN

1 Brought to light
2 Application
3 Beat generation device
4 Hemingway heroine
5 Chase of ballet fame
6 Not carved in stone
7 Ravel's *Introduction and Allegro*, e.g.
8 Analogy
9 Past
10 Chill out
11 Get
12 Battling
13 *The Sketch Book of Geoffrey Crayon,* ___
14 Work combiner
24 Craftsman Girolamo
25 Nice pet
26 Foil feature
27 Michael's *Zeppelin* costar
28 Dessert serving
29 Illegal block
30 Painter Salvator
31 Sun worshiper
32 Wrest
33 Sale item abbr.
35 Tackle moguls
37 How Nellie described herself
40 Cut off
41 Family
44 Literally, "bottle"
45 Hardly one
47 Emulated Tom
48 Contrived
49 Mount
50 Pinzón's command
51 Hot
52 Flurry
53 In ___ (A-Z)
54 Cows
55 Underdone

72

BY ERIC ALBERT

1

```
BATHWATER FACES
OTHERWISE ADLAI
REORIENTS ROARS
INLET TETRA INT
DOE SMELLED MII
ERST ERLES MANN
OED ESTRANGE
SEPTIC SAINTS
SIROCCOS TOE
ABEL AMUSE DRAB
DIM HIPPEST ADA
DLI ADARN OSCAR
EATAT RESENTING
STERE EMERGENCE
TESTS DONNAREED
```

7

```
ARABS SATSTILL
ROLLE LUSITANIA
ABATE ENTRANCED
ROM PRETEEN LOD
ACED AWARD HIVE
TODO GANN GONER
PALLORS POLERS
LAUD SLAY
ATMOST THATSIT
DRIPS SOOT EROS
HANS APORT EARL
ELI CRITTER NRA
RACEHORSE ALIEN
ELALAMEIN MEANT
SAMSPADE PONTS
```

13

```
MATURED PALMIST
ITERATE ALIENEE
STAGERS CANASTA
FACE ESCENT CTS
ICH ERRS HALE
THEA GROS TOPER
SERPENTS OILERS
PLUSSIGNS
SPELLS WREATHES
ERNES SORE SYST
NOGS TERI ASO
EPA BRIDGE BLED
CARTOON ADORING
ANDANTE TERENCE
SEERESS ENTREES
```

19

```
CAAN NASA
SURETO HOBART
SONORAN OMERTA
CURSING TEDDING
ARIS EBON ISNO
REPRO OOF ANTIS
FREEDOMOFSPEECH
FORESTERS
INHERITTHEEARTH
DEARS RUE SNARE
EAVE PIPP DCIX
STANNIC REDWINE
ARCANA ELAINES
STEROL SLICES
IRAN SASH
```

25

```
STAPLE FANATIC
IONIUM PICAYUNE
MRTAMBOURINEMAN
ITA PALMED SUBS
LUCK REPLY LOO
ARIES SKA ALTAR
REDRUM INACAST
MRSANDMAN
SNIGGLE ORATOR
STATE DAS DIANE
LAP AETNA SPED
ANIM DREAMY EPI
PLEASEMRPOSTMAN
PERGOLAS NEWARK
YESICAN GRANTS
```

31

```
PASTRIES DEPP
INCHARGE TAMARA
AERATION WRITES
SMILES SPOTLESS
TOPER GARB RTE
ENTS CATER KNOT
RES NOMINATIONS
COMMOTION
BLUDGEONING PEG
OOPS ANASS PINA
OCS GELS SALTI
MATAHARI BERLIN
ETALII SHOELACE
ROTTEN TEENAGER
REOS SPRAYERS
```

37

S	T	R	E	S	S	F	U	L		O	P	R	A	H
P	R	I	N	C	E	A	L	I		S	I	E	G	E
R	O	T	T	E	R	D	A	M		S	A	C	R	A
A	P	E		P	E	E	R	E	D		F	R	E	D
Y	E	S	I	T	I	S		R	I	B		E	E	R
			D	E	N		P	I	C	A		A	M	E
S	T	A	I	R		L	A	C	E	R	A	T	E	S
E	U	R	O		M	O	N	K	S		C	E	N	T
P	R	I	M	R	O	S	E	S		C	O	S	T	S
A	N	S		O	P	A	L		W	A	R			
R	S	T		Y	U	L		T	A	N	N	I	N	G
A	T	O	M		P	A	G	O	D	A		M	O	E
T	I	T	A	N		M	I	L	E	S	T	O	N	E
E	L	L	I	E		O	V	E	R	T	O	N	E	S
S	E	E	D	Y		S	E	T	S	A	D	A	T	E

43

H	E	L	I	O	P	H	O	B	E		S	E	A	S
O	P	E	N	S	E	A	S	O	N		T	A	U	T
T	A	N	G	L	E	W	O	O	D		O	G	R	E
L	U	I		O	K	S		K	E	R	P	L	O	P
I	L	E	T				K	A	I	S	E	R	S	
N	E	N	E		T	R	I	E	R	S		T	A	O
E	T	T	A		R	E	N	E		E	S	S	E	N
			S	O	A	P	O	P	E	R	A			
B	A	R	E	R		R	U	E	D		G	E	L	T
A	D	A		S	H	E	R	R	Y		E	M	I	R
T	E	N	T	O	E	S				T	O	N	I	
I	N	T	O	N	E	S		A	M	A		T	E	D
S	O	I	R		D	I	N	N	E	R	T	I	M	E
T	I	N	T		E	V	E	N	S	T	E	V	E	N
E	D	G	E		D	E	B	A	S	E	M	E	N	T

49

D	E	S	P	O	T	S		K	R	A	M	E	R	
E	Q	U	A	T	O	R		P	R	E	D	A	T	E
S	U	B	R	O	S	A		R	I	C	O	T	T	A
C	A	R	E	S	S		R	E	S	O	R	T	E	D
A	T	O		E	W	E		G	E	E	S	E		
R	I	G	A		S	H	A	R	O	N	S			
T	O	A	S	T		E	L	E	N	I		S	T	A
E	N	T	E	R	P	R	I	S	E	Z	O	N	E	S
S	S	E		A	T	E	S	T		E	D	E	N	S
			P	I	A	S	T	E	R		D	A	N	E
A	S	H	E	N		I	D	A		K	E	N		
T	H	O	R	A	C	I	C		T	A	O	I	S	T
R	I	S	I	B	L	E		C	H	I	N	E	S	E
A	R	E	O	L	A	S		P	E	R	U	S	E	R
P	E	N	D	E	D		O	R	E	S	T	E	S	

55

	C	E	R	E	S		S	P	I	G	O	T	S	
M	A	N	I	L	A		P	I	N	O	C	H	E	T
A	T	O	M	I	C		L	E	A	D	T	I	M	E
D	E	U	S		C	A	I	R	N	S		R	I	N
A	N	G		C	H	A	N	C	E		A	T	N	O
M	A	H	A	R	A	N	E	E		S	P	E	A	R
			N	E	R	D	S		T	A	P	E	R	S
	V	I	C	T	I	M		H	E	L	E	N	S	
N	A	T	H	A	N		R	E	N	T	A			
O	L	S	O	N		T	E	S	S	E	L	A	T	E
L	E	A	R		S	I	T	S	I	N		F	A	X
E	N	G		M	A	N	U	E	L		E	L	L	E
S	C	I	M	I	T	E	R		I	N	D	O	O	R
S	I	R	E	N	I	A	N		T	E	N	A	N	T
	A	L	G	I	E	R	S		Y	E	A	T	S	

61

J	A	Z	Z	A	G	E		S	E	A	A	I	R	
I	D	E	A	T	E	D		E	X	C	I	T	E	R
M	I	N	G	L	E	S		P	O	T	T	E	R	Y
E	P	I		S	E	D	A	N		R	A	D		
N	O	T	T	O		L	O	R	E		G	A	T	E
E	S	H	A	R	P		G	A	R	D	E	N	E	R
Z	E	S	T	I	E	R		T	A	I	N	T	S	
			A	G	R	O		E	T	R	E			
	M	I	M	I	C	S		D	E	G	R	A	D	E
D	O	M	I	N	E	E	R		D	E	A	R	E	R
R	A	M	S		N	M	E	X		S	L	A	T	E
A	N	O		T	A	P	E	D			B	E	C	
M	I	R	A	M	A	R		R	E	P	A	I	N	T
A	N	A	L	O	G	Y		E	L	E	V	A	T	E
	G	L	A	D	E	S		S	E	R	E	N	E	R

67

C	A	M	A	R	O	S		P	R	O	M	O	T	E
I	M	O	G	E	N	E		R	O	M	A	N	I	A
C	E	L	E	S	T	E		E	V	A	D	E	R	S
A	R	T		H	O	P	O	V	E	R		L	A	I
D	I	E	M		P	E	N	A	S		J	A	D	E
A	C	R	I	D		D	E	I		D	A	N	E	S
S	A	S	S	E	D		S	L	E	E	K	E	S	T
			S	T	A	R		S	E	G	A			
R	A	F	T	E	R	E	D		E	A	R	L	A	P
E	L	L	E	R		G	A	B		S	T	A	I	R
S	T	O	P		M	U	R	A	L		A	C	L	U
I	E	R		D	E	L	E	T	E	S		T	E	D
D	R	A	C	U	L	A		T	A	R	T	A	R	E
E	N	T	I	C	E	R		E	S	I	A	S	O	N
D	E	E	D	E	E	S		D	E	S	C	E	N	T

2

```
J A C Q U E L I N E ■ A C I D
I R R A T I O N A L ■ B A N E
G R O T E S Q U E S ■ U P T O
■ C A S E ■ I S A ■ S T O
I G O R ■ N A T ■ ■ R E A L
N E D ■ C H I ■ A E R I E S
U N I ■ R O D E N T S ■ N R A
R E L ■ A W E S O M E ■ K A L
E R E ■ V E S T R O N ■ A N T
S A D L E R ■ ■ M S T ■ N C O
■ T U E S ■ Z A P ■ B G E N
■ I N S ■ W O E ■ H O R A
S O D S ■ I M P R E S A R I O
K N E E ■ S E P A R A T O R S
I S E E ■ P R O F E S S O R S
```

8

```
A S B E S T O S ■ P R E W A R
R O A D T E S T ■ H E L E N E
D I S P E R S E ■ A S S A I L
O R K ■ P R O V O S T ■ S S A
R E E F ■ A B E L E ■ F E E T
S E T I N ■ U N E ■ S O L T I
■ N A R C S ■ H E R E T O
C H R I S T O P H E R W R E N
R I A T A S ■ I O N I A ■
E L I E L ■ G E M ■ F R E R E
V A N S ■ S A L E M ■ D U A L
A R T ■ S K Y B L U E ■ G P A
S I R R E E ■ E I N S T E I N
S T E E V E ■ R E G A I N E D
E Y E L E T ■ G R O U S E R S
```

14

```
G A M E B I R D ■ C L O P S
O R A T O R I O ■ T H E C A T
D E C A D E N T ■ R I V E R A
S O B ■ E N G A G E S ■ L A T
O L E S ■ E L R O Y ■ R O P E
N A T E S ■ E D O ■ B E T E L
■ S H A L I T S ■ Y E A S T Y
■ S E T S ■ C A L L ■
S T A L E S ■ C O W L I C K
O W N U P ■ P O L ■ A S H E S
L O N G ■ V E N O M ■ T O N E
A S U ■ R E T I R E S ■ R O N
C O L L I E ■ C A T T A I L S
E M A I L S ■ A D O A N N I E
S E R V E ■ L O O S E E N D
```

20

```
P I R A T E ■ B E S M E A R S
A C A R I D ■ A X L E T R E E
P E T A R D ■ G I A S C A L A
O R A T E ■ A N T I S ■ B I D
O U T ■ A L I E N ■ C I A O
S N A C K F O O D ■ S L A N G
E S T H E T E S ■ S C E N T ■
■ E Y E S ■ W H O A ■
■ C H E E R ■ C R O O N E R S
L O E S S ■ S H O R T S T O P
I N G E ■ S K A T E ■ O S E
S C I ■ S P I N E ■ A N N E E
B A R B A R I C ■ P L E I A D
O V A L T I N E ■ T O M A T O
N E S T E G G S ■ A T O N E S
```

26

```
■ D E S P O T ■ T O G G L E S
C O N C A V E ■ U P R A I S E
A C C U S E R ■ M E A T M A N
S T A T ■ R E T U R N ■ P U T
T O S S E D S A L A D S ■
I R E ■ R O A S T ■ S E W E R
G A M M A S ■ S S T ■ A A R E
A T E A S E ■ ■ I D L I N G
T E N T ■ S I C ■ D U S T E R
E S T E S ■ N O V A E ■ I S E
■ S U R V E I L L A N T S ■
P A C ■ M E A D O W ■ E G I S
A S H A M E D ■ L A S T O N E
S I A M E S E ■ A V E N U E S
A S P I R E D ■ S E N A T S
```

32

```
D E L T S ■ S C A R E C R O W
O V E R A ■ A L L A B R E V E
R I S O N ■ R E F R A I N E D
I N S T E P ■ M I E N ■ O R G
A C E ■ E M E E R ■ R U D I
■ E N V I R O N S ■ C A N O E
■ O N S E T ■ F E N C E S
■ M D C I I ■ A N G E S
M A R A C A ■ P U R S E ■
E C O L E ■ A R M R E S T S
M A P S ■ D R O P A ■ I T S
P R O ■ S E E S ■ R A B B I T
H O U S E B O A T ■ P A I G E
I N T E R A L I A ■ S W A M P
S I S T E R A C T ■ E L S A S
```

38

```
R E C E D E S   S P A R
E M O T I V E O N A D A T E
D E P O S E R H E A D P I N
S R A C R A N B E R R I E S
T I R E S   E R R   E D I E
A T E N   A R G O   A S S N
R U N T   F O O T E R S
  S T E P T O T H E R E A R
    R U S T I E R   D R E W
  F A T S   C A R O   T E A R
E L L A   S A T   D O A S I
D E L I N Q U E N C Y   C O T
H E I N O U S   A L L G O N E
S T E E L I E   G U A R D E R
  D R A B   S E N D E R S
```

44

```
B I O L O G I S T   S N E R T
A L L A T O N C E T O P E R
B E D C O V E R S A L I V E
A N O S E   I T E R A T E S
L E N   S H A V E N   S O R T
U S E S   A L E R T S   M E L
    E L L E N   H E L E N E
S A D C A F E   B R E A S T S
C R E T I N   P A A R S
A B C   C O S E L L   E S M E
L O I S   T I N K L Y   T U N
A R M A M E N T   E L A N D
B E A T A   B E R T L A N C E
L A T I N   A N A A L I C I A
E L E N I   D E N M O T H E R
```

50

```
  J E T S E T   B A L S A M
T A X R A T E   E D I T I O N
I N C E N S E   L A S A L L E
P I L E D   N E I G H   M I A
S T U   S W A Y Z E   M E E T
Y O D A   A G E E   G E N R E
  R E L A X E D   B E T T E R
    P H E R O M O N E
A C T I O N   C E N T R A L
P H O N Y   S T E N   S L O P
L A N E   S T O R E D   B O O
O N E   S T O R K   A B U T S
M C A L L E N   A R T E M I S
B E R E A V E   T I E L I N E
  S M I T E S   S P R A N G
```

56

```
R O S E S   F A M I S H E S
E N I A C   P O L E V A U L T
S E N T A   E A S T E R N E R
I O U   P I L L A R S   L A O
N C O   E N T I C E   S I N K
G A S P   K I N E   P E K O E
S T E A M I N G   M I N E R
    D O N G   L O N I
  F A R E D   M O N G O L I A
M O R E S   J A V A   R I N G
E R R S   C O L E C O   M A E
A L I   C A R L S O N   I L L
L O V E L Y D A Y   A R T I E
I R E N E C A R A   L I E N S
E N D T O E N D   L O D E S
```

62

```
W A S P   S P A C E B A R
A R T O O   S P A R E T I M E
T R E E R   A L I E N A T E S
T A R   C A B I N E T   P R O
E I N   S P I C E D   B A I L
A G E D   O N E S   F O R C E
U N S E E D E D   R I A T A S
    G R A S   G E L S
S A C R A L   B E D S T E A D
C L U E S   L A S S   S A N E
R A R E   D A L T O N   R C A
E D S   P I C K A X E   S I D
E D I T O R I A L   A S H E S
D I V E R G E N T   R H O N E
S N E A K E R S   E T T A
```

68

```
M A S C A R A   B E A T S
A M P U L E S   I N D I C I A
D A R T E R S   S C O P I N G
E S E   S U A V E   S P E A R
I S A S   N I E C E   I N R E
R E D U X   L I T R E   C U E
A D S O R B   L E V E R E T S
    M A W S   D I R E
T E R I Y A K I   L I A B L E
A X E   S N I D E   E R R E D
S P C A   A P E S T   S E A M
T O R U S   P E D R O   A K U
E R U D I T E   R A M E K I N
S T I R R E R   A M E R I N D
  T A K E S   S P R I N G S
```

3

```
RUMPLES    SIGMA
ATALANTA  TETRAD
DOGOODER  OUTONA
APE  SORTERS  ADP
RING  FEIGNS  NET
SATAN  SERA  DELE
 SARAH  REDCEDAR
  ISIS  TORT
CRASHPAD  SORES
LASH  BLOC  COMTE
AGT  NOUGAT  POEM
PTO  INTERIM  TRI
PIRATE  ALLURING
EMILES  RODLAVER
DEALS    SEEHERE
```

9

```
COVENANT  GASKET
OPERATOR  ACTIVE
DEROGATE  MEANER
ENOS  NEEDED  GRR
DEN   SORT  ASI
 RAHAL  FEED  NIE
  ALASKA  ARDOR
BEAUTYANDBRAINS
LASSO  MOSAIC
USS  SCOW  SNELL
EEE  HALS   IAN
NIN  MANETS  ASTO
ENTAIL  DETESTED
STELAE  GREATONE
SOREST  ENTRANTS
```

15

```
 FELIPE  SOLOMON
SIMENON  PUERILE
TRANCES  ENSURES
RENO  NIECE  RAT
AMA  PRANCE  FOTO
PATRIARCH  FIRER
SNEAKIER  ALOSS
  MESSENGER
 SPARE  AIREDALE
WARDS  ASPERSION
AREA  CREPES  RCA
GAS  DONDI  SLAT
ELUSIVE  EREMITE
REMOVES  SHRINES
SEEDERS  TORTES
```

21

```
STATEMENT  LIRA
OHIORIVER  SUMER
DISPARAGE  ELMER
ISLES  SAMMALONE
UBER  SITOUT  RGS
MESS  HOERS  STAT
  BOND  STAGE
SPROUTS  STEELED
TEENY  SAAR
ENES  SMEWS  WOOL
LCD  WHELPS  ANCE
LIPREADER  PLATO
ALIEN  UNITARIAN
TEPID  SINECURVE
EDEN  ACTRESSES
```

27

```
 CIDE  MANIPLE
 COVEYS  INASEAT
GAMESETANDMATCH
OLEG  DECOR  EKE
OLIOS  ACRE  BREL
NINTENDO  ALEAD
INT  WEIRD  ANN
EGO  SEEDERS  DPS
 OSU  RICES  TRU
SNAPS  NOBOTHER
CAEN  ENGR  SIEVE
AIS  EATUP  TWIT
BLOODFROMASTONE
LOWPAID  SPILLS
ERNESTS  ALEF
```

33

```
 DOCTOR  GERBER
DEVIATE  ADORNED
ELEANOR  RICARDO
CIR  SEURAT  COUP
OMAN  SNUG  DEUCE
RIGOR  SMITE  TER
STEREO  INHALERS
 MALINGERS
CATALINA  MIMOSA
ALS  LOFTS  EFREM
SCARY  ROTS  TIME
TORE  SARAHS  GIN
EVICTOR  GARLAND
SESTINE  ENIGMAS
 STONED  YESSIR
```

39

```
A U T O G I R O S   B O S C
I R E N E C A R A   B A N T A
M A T U R A T E S   U L C E R
E N O S   R A G S E L L E R S
D I N   V E T O I N G   O N E
  A S H E   A N E T   U V E A
    E R S T   R I C H E S T
T O L I V E     C O U R T S
E V A D E R S   R E A R
S E P I   A H M E   S A L T
T R I   S P R I C H T   O A F
A N D D I E I N L A   S A K I
B E A R D   F O U R L A N E R
L A R A S   T A S T I N E S S
E T Y M   S N E E Z E D A T
```

45

```
  C O S T A   L A M I N A
G I B L E T S   E L E V E N S
R E L I A N T   N I N E V E H
O N I T   O R A N G E   A M O
P E G   I C O N   O D O R
E G O S   O P E N   P L A N T
D A R K A G E S   M A I N E
    E R R S   K E R N
  B U T T E   D I M A G G I O
N A N C Y   H O M O   O U S T
I N C H   S U M O   T O T
G A L   A P R O N S   I L L E
E N A B L E R   O N A T E A R
L A S A G N A   S A D I S T S
  S P L A S H   P O S S E
```

51

```
S C R A B B L E   C H E E R
P R E T E R I T   H O R R O R
A U T O D A F E   O R N A T E
R E I M S   E R V I N   S A D
E T E S   A B N E R   C U R B
S S S   F L O A T   M A R I O
    I T A L   C A R E E N
D R A G N E T   F I N E S S E
R O L L E R   G O N G
A T L A S   F R O D O   D A L
S T E M   P I E T Y   G I S H
T E L   V E G A N   P R E S A
I N U R E S   S O C R A T E S
C L I E N T   E T C E T E R A
Y A X I S   D E S S E R T S
```

57

```
J U R A S S I C   H R S
I N A C T I V E   C O O E R
V A N H A L E N   A R M P I T
E G G   L O S T I N S P A C E
D E E R E   E R S E   R O T
  D S O   E T R E   L A T H
  M A R I O   P L A T T E
T H E M A N O F T H E Y E A R
W A X E R S   G O D E L
E R A L   A R T S   O R R
R P M   S P C A   D W E E B
P O P U L A R V O T E   M I A
S O L V E R   I T A L I A N S
  N E E D S   T O R T O N I S
  S A S   Y E S A N D N O
```

63

```
J U R Y R I G   S P R I N G S
O N E T I M E   P L A T E A U
H U D D L E R   L A N T E R N
N S F   L E M M I N G   D O S
D U O S   T A I N T   C I T E
O A R E D   N O T   R H E T T
E L D E R L Y   S Q U A R E S
    P A Y   U S S
S P E A K E R   S I T S P A T
T I N G E   E T A   S E R R A
E T T E   D D A Y S   D I B S
P S I   F E R R I T E   M I T
S T T E I L O   N A R R A T E
T O L E D O S   G R I F T E R
O P E R O S E   S E E K E R S
```

69

```
B A M A   L A N D C R A B S
E V A N S   A L F A R O M E O
D I R G E   D A L M A T I A N
L A C   P A Y M E N T   A N N
A T O   T U B E R S   A B I E
M E N U   S I D S   F I L E T
  S I N A T R A   D U R E S S
    L O R D   R E M S
S T H E N O   S O B E A T S
C E A S E   S M U T   C H O P
R A T S   S E I N E D   E M I
E T E   B L A D D E R   F E N
W I D E R A N G E   I D I O T
E M I N E N C E S   P O R N O
D E T E R G E N T   A M E S
```

4

```
MOTES CARDSHARP
APART OVEREAGER
TINEA REQUISITE
IND BARNUMS TAT
LIES SAGES SAKE
DOMICILES LATEX
ANSARA STRIDENT
MENS SOBS
ACCESSED TEASES
COAST PENALCODE
ARNE SABOT KNIT
ROT CARAMEL AFT
INAMORATA UNTIL
DETONATED GRACE
STARKNESS EASES
```

10

```
MICA BLANKETED
UCANT RICEARONI
TEENA INTERIORS
ABSOLUTE ECLAT
NOU CRANIAL AGA
TART BISON STEN
STARMAN STALEST
IAN IRE
DABBLES DAMPERS
ISEE LIFER TROT
SCH LYRICAL UTA
PRATE ARBORDAY
LIVEALONE WAITE
ABERRANCE ESTER
YESINDEED HESS
```

16

```
HAMOMELET APSIS
AMERICANA DEERE
CASANOVAS IDIOM
ETONS ECT PANNE
KING ENTER LESS
SSS DUDEDUP NIT
HARED SECEDE
BABIYAR THEATER
ALAMOS SHELL
RIC FIGURES FCC
BETS ARLES COAL
ANEMO ATE KARMA
RARER TAPDANCES
ATILT INLANDERS
SEATS SAYSAYSAY
```

22

```
SPEEDBUMP WAF
EASTERNER GAILS
INTONABLE ARRET
SPININESS RIDEA
MIV STL SADSACK
SPAR STEELE TEE
ELAM DRINKERS
RECESSION
TIRESOME FOOL
ORU SHILOH BRIM
COSTING NEH SCI
ONTHE REFRESHED
MALES ANIMATING
EGEST TOLERANCE
ERE ELMSTREET
```

28

```
STREAMER SHOES
HAIRLINE HEARTS
ENDGAMES ASSURE
ALE NEREIDS DIV
RIFTS GAVE PIKE
ENOS AYLA BITER
REROOT SNARLERS
NUTS ARES
SEAGRAPE LANCES
ARRAS EXPO EBRO
TAIS ONCE ERROL
ISA ANTENNA ADA
REDONE EPISODIC
ERNANI DATELINE
SETAN SLEDDOGS
```

34

```
BARRISTER IPSE
ONEORMORE CAROL
DIALTONES ANELE
EMIL GAMETE MIC
DARIN LIVEN ITT
COT TENS EAR
SICKER ERS TRIO
ALLELES SOTHERN
CLAD ATT REESES
RAS STAR SAD
ITS TENAM REBUS
SEA ADDLED SINE
TACKY PANATELLA
ASTAS ALANARKIN
NEST TATERTOTS
```

40

```
J A M E S J O N E S ■ ■ F I T
E L E C T O R A T E S ■ ■ I V Y
A L L T O G E T H E R ■ ■ J A N
N E T ■ A S S ■ A S I N I N E
E V E S ■ ■ ■ A N D S O ■ ■ ■
T I D E ■ B A S S O ■ A L F
T A D P O L E S ■ U S H E R
E T O ■ R E S O R B S ■ S E G
■ E W E R S ■ R E L E A S E R
■ S N L ■ S E T A E ■ U C L A
■ ■ A L E C S ■ ■ S H A Y
T O R N A D O ■ E F G ■ A N N
O B I ■ M A L E V O L E N C E
W I T ■ P R E F E R E N C E S
N E Z ■ ■ E S T R A N G E R S
```

46

```
C O R F U ■ P R I S M A T I C
A V E R S ■ R A N K & F I L E
R E P O T ■ E S T I M A T E S
A R U ■ E L S T E R ■ R O U T
B & B ■ D E S E R T S ■ S M A
I D L E ■ T U R N S U P ■ ■
N O I R ■ M P S ■ L O C H S
E N C A S E ■ ■ M U S L I M
R E A T A ■ S R O ■ S A D A
■ ■ O N E S T E P ■ E S E L
S K I ■ A R E A R U G ■ S & L
H A N A ■ I X T A P A ■ A S A
A P A T H E T I C ■ R I C E R
H U N T & P E C K ■ T O T E M
S T E A R A T E S ■ H U S K S
```

52

```
S M A R T E N E D ■ A S S E T
H O L E I N O N E ■ M E A L S
O V E N M I T T S ■ A P N E A
P E R ■ E D I E S ■ H A G A R
P I T H S ■ O N E L ■ L A N I
E N S E ■ E N T R A P ■ R O N
■ ■ A L S ■ E T C E T E R A
■ P I R A T E ■ S E R I E S ■
S A N D I E S T ■ R E D ■ ■
P U N ■ R E S E W S ■ A P E D
A L O P ■ S A R A ■ P L A N E
R E V E L ■ Y E N T A ■ L T S
S T A T E ■ I N T E R A L I A
E T T A S ■ S C O R E C A R D
R E E L S ■ T E N N E S S E E
```

58

```
H E Y J U D E ■ D E D U C T S
A Q U A R I A ■ E R A S U R E
N U M B I N G ■ M I N A R E T
S A M ■ S A L T I N E ■ S A T
O T I S ■ H E H ■ ■ S P I T E
L O E W E ■ T E C H ■ E V E R
O R R I N ■ ■ S P A N N E D
■ ■ L L E W E L L Y N ■ ■
■ M A L A R I A ■ ■ S I D L E
S A D E ■ A L S O ■ E N R O L
T R A D E ■ O R A ■ G E N E
I Q S ■ L I O N I Z E ■ A G A
G U T C A L L ■ O T T O M A N
M E R I T E D ■ L E T M E G O
A Z A L E A S ■ E C U A D O R
```

64

```
F A S T L A N E ■ P E R M I T
E V E R Y M A N ■ A L D E N S
M A R I N A R A ■ A M A N D A
A L A T E ■ C B E R S ■ H O R
L O P E ■ C O L A S ■ M A L I
E N E ■ C U T E R ■ L A D E S
■ ■ R A M I S ■ H A V E N T
S A T A N I C ■ R E G E N T S
A L A N O N ■ D E M O N ■ ■
F A C I E ■ P O P E S ■ S O D
E C O N ■ L O G A N ■ S H U E
N A B ■ C A P E R ■ A M I S S
E R E B U S ■ A T A L A N T A
S T L U K E ■ R E S I S T E D
S E L L E R ■ S E A S H O R E
```

70

```
M I K E S H E N K ■ S C O T T
E R I K S A T I E ■ C A P R A
N O N E N T I T Y ■ O N E U P
A N D S ■ C O R N ■ R E N E W
C E E ■ C H L O E I N ■ M B A
E R R O R ■ O U S T ■ M I L T
■ ■ R I G G S ■ A V E N U E
P O T T E R Y ■ B L A N D E R
A U R O R A ■ S E O U L ■ ■
S T A N ■ N O W A ■ L O T T A
S S S ■ A T W O R S T ■ A R R
O C H E R ■ L O A N ■ C H I S
V O C A L ■ I S R A E L I T E
E R A S E ■ S I M P L E T O N
R E N T S ■ H E S S O F I N E
```

5

```
B I R D . W I S E R . T R A
O U N C E . A S I D E . R E S
V I T A L S T A T I S T I C S
A L E . L A C . O C T A G O N
. D R J . G H E N T . B O N .
P A N E S . O S T . T O N . .
A B A B E I N T H E W O O D S
I L L . I T T H E R E . M I A
R E A P S T H E H A R V E S T
. . F U M . E T O . P I T A S
. A F R . F R E T S . A R F .
I N A R U S H . S O D . I F A
S W I S S T I M E P I E C E S
P A R . I O N I A . S L A C K
Y R S . S P E N T . K I L T .
```

11

```
A V E R A G E . A B D U C T S
T A X I C A B . E A R H A R T
T R E S T L E . S T I F L E R
A I R E . O R A T E . . L E A
C A T . A I T C H . P A I L S
K N E L L S . C E L E S T E S
S T R E P . P O T E N T A T E
. . . V I R U L E N C E . . .
M A R I N A R A S . I R M A S
O P E N E Y E D . A L S A C E
U P P E R . B E R G S . D E M
S R A . U R S A E . S E T A .
S I S T I N E . I N H U M A N
E S T A T E D . S T O M A T A
S E E R E S S . A S T O N E S
```

17

```
O C E A N S T A T E . . T A P
N A V R A T I L O V A . O S U
O R A N G E S O D A S . L I P
U N D O . W A N D . I D E A S
R E E L . . E L I N O R . . .
. . D A N . L E N . N A S H .
. R E P R O . Y R S . K N E E
H O T A I R . . I C E C A P .
O P E L . O T B . D O Y E N .
P E R M . O R E . E E K . . .
. . N E W M A N . . O H N O .
S H A R I . L A M P . N A I L
E E L . C R A Z Y E I G H T S
A L L . K I L I M A N J A R O
S P Y . G A R Y L A R S O N .
```

23

```
S C R A B B L E . C O B R A S
T O O D L E O O . O R I E N T
I N S E A S O N . N E G A T E
E T E . M I S S E D . O L E S
S E N S E D . . L O S T I N .
. . . P R E G N A N T . T A D
O D O R S . O U T E R . I V E
D A V Y . T E R I S . K E E N
A M E . G E S S O . K I S S Y
Y A R . I N P E N C I L . . .
. S T A T E R . A N N A L S .
S C A N . M O U R N S . G E T
H E X A D E . T E A M M A T E
O N E M A N . E N D E A V O R
D E S E R T . S E A N P E N N
```

29

```
A L L O W I N . M I A S M A S
D I O R A M A . O N L E A V E
I N V A D E R . P E T E R E D
P E E . S T R I P E S . I R A
O M A R . . A W E D . S E A T
S A N E R . S A D . S T A G E
E N D S O F . S U M M O N E D
. . M I T E R . P A I N T . .
S H A D O W E D . A R I O S E
W A R E S . C I C . K N I T S
A I R S . R O S H . G N A T .
D R I . M A R C O N I . E R R
D I A M O N D . R I C O T T A
L E G A T E E . A L E R T L Y
E R E C T E D . L E S S E E S
```

35

```
S T R E E T S . H O O P L A .
T R U S T E E . E N D E A R S
K U M Q U A T . R A I N M A N
I D O . I S T O M I N . B B A
T E R O . E L D E R . F A I R
T A E L S . E D T . K O D A K
S U D D E N . S I C H U A N .
. . . M E A D . C O A L . . .
. S P A T T E R . E N O U G H
M A R I O . G Y P . S U N R A
A R I D . T R A I T . T I E R
R A M . O R A N G E S . T A D
S C A L P E D . P R O M I S E
H E R O I N E . E N L I V E N
. N Y M E T S . N E S T E R S
```

41

```
CHESSMAN  STASIS
HEREWEGO  HAVENT
EMANATES  AMANDA
MIS PANICLE SER
ITALS DEAL CENT
SOBE BARB BUSTS
ENLACES SAUL
  EERIE  CROWD
  NAST CANTHIS
CAMEO EGAD TISH
ACED MEET SETTO
LAT PINNATE EAR
ICEDIN ELEPHANT
FIRING VARIANCE
SASSES ANNASTEN
```

47

```
MAGENTA SAGUARO
IBERIAN PHONIER
NOTABIT HALFMAD
GLOSS ILE FELLA
LINE BLORE DELI
EST SOLVENT SON
SHOETREE FOISTS
   CROSSWORD
INROAD TORTILLA
MAO DIVORCE EAR
ITCH NURSE FORT
TAKES LYE HINDI
ASIATIC ORIGINS
THERESA FISHNET
EASTMAN FOSTERS
```

53

```
STRATAS ZEBRA
PHONETAG INVERT
RESEMBLE NODDER
IFE PALATES PAY
TOTS TERR SIRS
ENTER SAS ANUT
ZAFTIG DOGLEG
EERO EARL
PURSES SPOILT
BENI SPA WEARE
LTDS EROS SPAM
ORE TALENTS BIB
NORMAL NEOPRENE
DUGOUT AURICLED
SOTTO PENATES
```

59

```
SCRABBLE REBUS
OLIVEOIL TONONE
REVENGED RETOSS
EVERS SEMIS MEA
SERT ADROP STEM
TRA STOLE OCOME
  SHOWY GROWLS
JOHANN BRAWNY
REVILE FRILL
IRENE ZOOMS WAN
BORE DORKY PELE
ABC NIOBE BEALE
LOOPER INCENSED
DAMASK DURACELL
SMELT SPIKELEE
```

65

```
CROSSFIRE ATSEA
LEVITATED DREDS
AMERICANINDIANS
UAR FILENE TOE
SIC FEY BAILORS
ENOL OUTPOSTS
NEH ORR ASHOE
JIFFY PEG NEINS
UNITE AAH AIN
MCDONALD TIMS
PREFACE REB NOM
SEN ASMILE GTE
FATHERCONFESSOR
OSLIN ENGINEERS
REYES STONEWASH
```

71

```
TICKLERS ARCHER
ETHIOPIA PARADE
TRUSSING EREBUS
RANSACKS MEDICI
ANGELES MARITAL
DAN BUN TATI
AVE MELON DOBIE
LENTO ARC ORLON
CHRIS GAHAN ENT
HEAR LEX UNU
EMPEROR CRANKED
METIER PAIRWISE
INURED ENCEINTE
SCROLL TALENTED
TEENSY SLEDDERS
```

6

```
QUARTERS   AFR
UNCERTAIN  BLAST
ONTHEEDGE  BUTTE
TARA SING  ARIAN
EMEND OSSA RONS
MES ELMO   PRINCE
EDS ALEF   REESES
   IDONTMIND
BARNEY HILT  BAS
AROUND ELSE  ACT
GRIN SATE  DONEE
GILDS PIPS DATE
EVIAN EMOTIONAL
DENTI DESECRATE
  GET  STRESSED
```

12

```
STANDFAST  MAJOR
HONORARIA  AGAPE
ORALEXAMS  DRIED
ONT DEBIT  DEANS
IOOS SILED  ELIE
NULLS AESOP  ANA
STEEPENS  MRBIG
  PADS  PEAL
 PETRI MASTIFFS
LAB STEEN  ENOLA
ORBS SOLON  IRED
CATHY LARAM  TED
ADIEU INAMINUTE
LODER TIMELINES
EXERT HEADSTART
```

18

```
CROSSWORD TATAR
HARPERLEE EMOTE
IMPATIENS DELTA
VOID TATIES  DEC
ANNES TERN  MAST
SEE SWEDES  ALTO
   ITIS DUSTIER
ASHCAN  RATERS
THEOREM GELS
HORN VISORS  GAS
LEOS ASTI  ATARI
ELI STERNO  AMEN
TANTE DOGRACING
ICENT IVANLENDL
CESTA TETEATETE
```

24

```
MUSSING  SEARCH
ERECTOR BUSFARE
KARASEA INSIDER
ANIMALMAGNETISM
TIE SAMMY   OTI
EASTS TEO  LAMIT
  EATON COVENS
 RANDOMDRAWING
POISON METES
LURES PED  ROMAN
ENE FINCH   AGO
ADDEDATTRACTION
SLAVETO OPHELIA
EELIEST SPARING
STELMO  SYRINGE
```

30

```
 GOESSLOW AFACT
VERSATILE PAULA
ORANGEMEN SITAR
CATES BACHELORS
ARES METERS  CIA
LDS CARESS  DANL
  FARES  AIDES
 MARTYR BASKET
LIMES  DANTE
UNIT GOINTO  GMS
MCL DENOTE  TRAM
BELVEDERE OHARE
APIAN DAREDEVIL
RIOTS AMENDMENT
SENSE YARDSALE
```

36

```
REDDEST  ARMADA
ISRAELI CUEBALL
STARRED ESTELLE
KOP DIR  SHALES
ENID SEEA  MIGS
DINES DALAI  ERE
 AGEES LABRADOR
 RETAINERS
SWEEPERS SEPIA
COM SNITS  GENRE
ROUT DIPS  NITA
ILLEST CEA  TIS
BEARCAT EGOTIST
ENTRAPS DEVIATE
SEABEE  STALLER
```

42

```
  S O A P       P L U S
  B U N G E E   F I A S C O
K A R A O K E   R A N S A C K
E L F   N O R M A N D   M A E
A L A S   E I E I O   U P S Y
N A C H O   E L L   K N E E S
  D E I S T   S T I R F R Y
    I T E R   Y S E R
  G A T E L E G   A B O R T
A S T E R   D A H   S C O U T
R T E S   L L O Y D   K O L A
C A L   B O I L E R S   T S E
H A I T I A N   N A T U R A L
  D E B A T E   A M A Z O N
    R A S H       S N I T
```

48

```
T H E T I M E S   R E V E R E
H E R A L I B I   E D A M E S
A M E R I C A N   D I R E C T
T A L   A S N E R   T I R E R
S T O O D   W E B   A I D A
M I N G   S T Y L U S   T E D
E N G L A N D   N E V A D A
      E R O S   A C T I
P I N D A R   C H A R M E R
A M A   T E E P E E   T O P O
R O N S   S N O   T U N I S
A G E N T   D I N A H   O C S
D E T E R S   R O M A N C E S
E N T R E E   O N E T O O N E
S E E D E R   T E X A S T E A
```

54

```
S C A R E D O F   C H A R S
A L C A P O N E   B A I L E E
F A C T O R E D   A T T I C A
A R E   S I M O O N S   G I S
R I D S   C A R A S   A N T I
I C E U P   N A S   S N E A D
S E D G E S   S T R A D D L E
    A R A L   S I L O
A M E R I C A S   C A R M E L
N O V E L   C P A   D R I V E
D R E D   T E E T H   A L I S
R A N   B O R N E U P   E N S
E V I L E R   C A R A P A C E
W I N E R Y   E S T R O G E N
S A G A N   R E S T L E S S
```

60

```
L E E I A C O C C A   W H O
O R A N G E J U I C E   H E N
G A R D E N S T A T E   A X E
I S T O   S I L O   C S T
C E O   P U M A S   L I Z
    C A R P S   W I S E D
  A R T I S   A R A P A H O
I N F E R N O   L I S P I N G
F O R E I G N   A C H E D
S T I P E   A N E E D
  I K E   A R P A D   A D A
  A R S   L I A R   S P A N
B E A   A R I S T O C R A C Y
I A N   L A K E O N T A R I O
B U S   T E N N I S S T A R
```

66

```
B U S T E D U P   H E I F E R
O N E O N O N E   O C T A V E
O R A L T E S T   C R O N E S
T I D E S   H A I K U   D A T
E P O S   G O L D S   C A R L
D E G   M O R S E   S O N D E
    C O I N   S E A N C E S
R E W A R N   P R E E N S
A V E R A G E   B E G S
R A L L Y   T H R E E   P U G
E L L A   A N A I S   T U N E
N U B   G R A S S   B I L B O
E A R F U L   S T A R T L E D
S T E R N E   A L K A L I N E
S E D A N S   R E A G E N T S
```

72

```
B U B B L E S   P O R T A G E
A S A R U L E   A L E R T E R
R A T E C A P   R D L A I N G
E G O T I S T   A D A P T T O
D E N T A T E   L A X
    I T A L Y   C H E F
C R I T I C   M E S S H A L L
L O N E R   C A L   K A F K A
I S C A R I O T   K I T T E N
P A A R   S C I F I
    A O K   I N S H A P E
S T A R T L E   A S T O R I A
T O W A W A Y   S M O K I N G
I T E R A T E   C E L E S T E
R O S E R E D   O N E Y E A R
```

ALSO AVAILABLE

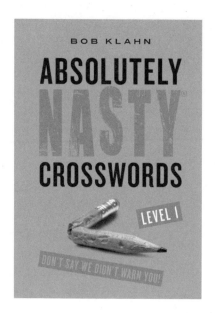

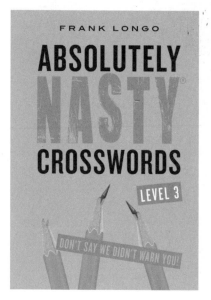

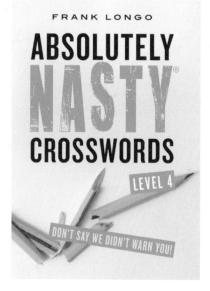